Youth And Sex

By
Mary Scharlieb

Youth And Sex

CHAPTER I.

CHANGES OBSERVABLE DURING PUBERTY AND ADOLESCENCE IN GIRLS.

1. Changes in the Bodily Framework.—During this period the girl's skeleton not only grows remarkably in size, but is also the subject of well-marked alterations and development. Among the most evident changes are those which occur in the shape and inclination of the pelvis. During the years of childhood the female pelvis has a general resemblance to that of the male, but with the advent of puberty the vertical portion of the hip bones becomes expanded and altered in shape, it becomes more curved, and its inner surface looks less directly forward and more towards its fellow bone of the other side. The brim of the pelvis, which in the child is more or less heart-shaped, becomes a wide oval, and consequently the pelvic girdle gains considerably in width. The heads of the thigh bones not only actually, in consequence of growth, but also relatively, in consequence of change of shape in the pelvis, become more widely separated from each other than they are in childhood, and hence the gait and the manner of running alters greatly in the adult woman. At the same time the angle made by the junction of the spinal column with the back of the pelvis, known as the sacro-vertebral angle, becomes better marked, and this also contributes to the development of the characteristic female type. No doubt the female type of pelvis can be recognised in childhood, and even before birth, but the differences of male and female pelves before puberty are so slight that it requires the eye of an expert to distinguish them. The very remarkable differences that are found between the adult male and the adult female pelvis begin to appear with puberty and develop rapidly, so that no one could mistake the pelvis of a properly developed girl of sixteen or eighteen years of age for that of a boy. These differences are due in part to the action of the muscles and ligaments on the growing bones, in part to the weight of the body from above and the reaction of the ground from beneath, but they are also largely due to the growth and development of the internal organs peculiar to the woman. All these organs exist in the

normal infant at birth, but they are relatively insignificant, and it is not until the great developmental changes peculiar to puberty occur that they begin to exercise their influence on the shape of the bones. This is proved by the fact that in those rare cases in which the internal organs of generation are absent, or fail to develop, there is a corresponding failure in the pelvis to alter into the normal adult shape. The muscles of the growing girl partake in the rapid growth and development of her bony framework. Sometimes the muscles outgrow the bones, causing a peculiar lankiness and slackness of figure, and in other girls the growth of the bones appears to be too rapid for the muscles, to which fact a certain class of "growing pain" has been attributed.

Another part of the body that develops rapidly during these momentous years is the bust. The breasts become large, and not only add to the beauty of the girl's person, but also manifestly prepare by increase of their glandular elements for the maternal function of suckling infants.

Of less importance so far as structure is concerned, but of great importance to female loveliness and attractiveness, are the changes that occur in the clearing and brightening of the complexion, the luxuriant growth, glossiness, and improved colour of the hair, and the beauty of the eyes, which during the years which succeed puberty acquire a new and singularly attractive expression.

The young girl's hands and feet do not grow in proportion with her legs and arms, and appear to be more beautifully shaped when contrasted with the more fully developed limb.

With regard to the internal organs, the most important are those of the pelvis. The uterus, or womb, destined to form a safe nest for the protection of the child until it is sufficiently developed to maintain an independent existence, increases greatly in all its dimensions and undergoes certain changes in shape; and the ovaries, which are intended to furnish the ovules, or eggs (the female contribution towards future human beings), also develop both in size and in structure.

Owing to rapid growth and to the want of stability of the young girl's tissues, the years immediately succeeding puberty are not only those of rapid physiological change, but they are those during which irreparable damage may be done unless those who have the care of young girls understand what these dangers are, how they are produced, and how they may be averted.

With regard to the bony skeleton, lateral curvature of the spine is, in mild manifestation, very frequent, and is too common even in the higher degrees. The chief causes of this deformity are:

(1) The natural softness and want of stability in the rapidly growing bones and muscles;

(2) The rapid development of the bust, which throws a constantly increasing burden on these weakened muscles and bones; and

(3) The general lassitude noticeable amongst girls at this time which makes them yield to the temptation to stand on one leg, to cross one leg over the other, and to write or read leaning on one elbow and bending over the table, whereas they ought to be sitting upright. Unless constant vigilance is exerted, deformity is pretty sure to occur—a deformity which always has a bad influence over the girl's health and strength, and which, in those cases where it is complicated by the pathological softness of bones found in cases of rickets, may cause serious alteration in shape and interfere with the functions of the pelvis in later life.

2. Changes in the Mental Nature.—These are at least as remarkable as the changes in the bodily framework. There is a slight diminution in the power of memorising, but the faculties of attention, of reasoning, and of imagination, develop rapidly. Probably the power of appreciation of the beautiful appears about this time, a faculty which is usually dormant during childhood. More especially is this true with regard to the beauty of landscape; the child seldom enjoys a landscape as such, although isolated beauties, such as that of flowers, may sometimes be appreciated.

As might be anticipated, all things are changing with the child during these momentous years: its outlook on life, its appreciation of other people and of itself, alter greatly and continuously. The wonderfully rapid growth and alterations in structure of the generative organs have their counterpart in the mental and moral spheres; there are new sensations which are scarcely recognised and are certainly not understood by the subject: vague feelings of unrest, ill-comprehended desires, and an intense self-consciousness take the place of the unconscious egoism of childhood.

The processes of Nature as witnessed in the season of spring have their counterpart in the changes that occur during the early years of adolescence. The earth warmed by the more direct rays of the sun and softened by recurring showers is transformed in a few weeks from its bare and dry winter garb into the wonderful beauty of spring. This yearly miracle fails to impress us as it should do because we have witnessed it every year of our lives, and so, too, the great transformation from child to budding woman fails to make its appeal to our understanding and sympathy because it is of so common occurrence. If it were possible for adults to really remember their own feelings and aspirations in adolescent years, or if it were possible for us with enlightened sympathy to gain access to the enchanted garden of youth, we should be more adequate guides for the boys and girls around us. As it is we entirely fail to appreciate the heights of their ambitions, hopes, and joys, and we have no measure with which to plumb the depths of their fears, their disappointments, and their doubts. The transition between radiant joy and confident hope in the future to a miserable misinterpretation of sensations both physical and psychical are rapid. It is the unknown that is terrible to us all, and to the child the changes in its body, the changes in its soul and spirit, which we pass by as commonplace, are full of suggestions of abnormality, of disaster, and of death. Young people suffer much from the want of comprehension and intelligent sympathy of their elders, much also from their own ignorance and too fervid imagination. The instability of the bodily tissues and the variability of their functions find a counterpart in the instability of the mental and moral natures and in the variability of their phenomena. Adolescents indeed "never continue in one stay;" left to themselves they will begin many pursuits, but persevere with, and finish, nothing.

Youth is the time for rapidly-succeeding friends, lovers, and heroes. The schoolfellow or teacher who is adored to-day may become the object of indifference or even of dislike to-morrow. Ideas as to the calling or profession to be adopted change rapidly, and opinions upon religion, politics, &c., vary from day to day. It is little wonder that there is a special type of adolescent insanity differing entirely from that of later years, one in which, owing to the want of full development of mental faculties, there are no systematised delusions, but a rapid change from depression and melancholy to exaltation bordering on mania. Those parents and guardians who know something of the peculiar physical and mental conditions of adolescence will be best prepared both to treat the troubles wisely, and by sympathy to help the young people under their care to help themselves.

One of the phenomena of adolescence is the dawn of the sexual instinct. This frequently develops without the child knowing or understanding what it means. More especially is this true of young girls whose home life has been completely sheltered, and who have not had the advantage, or disadvantage, of that experience of life which comes early to those who live in crowded tenements or amongst the outspoken people of the countryside. The children of the poorer classes have, in a way, too little to learn: they are brought up from babyhood in the midst of all domestic concerns, and the love affairs of their elders are intimately known to them, therefore quite early in adolescence "ilka lassie has her laddie," and although the attraction be short-lived and the affection very superficial, yet it is sufficient to give an added interest to life, and generally leads to an increased care in dress and an increased desire to make the most of whatever good looks the girl may possess. The girl in richer homes is probably much more bewildered by her unwonted sensations and by the attraction she begins to feel towards the society of the opposite sex.

Probably in these days, when there is more intermingling of the sexes, the girl's outlook is franker, and, so far as this is concerned, healthier, than it was forty or fifty years ago. It is very amusing to elders to hear a boy scarcely in his teens talking of "his best girl," or to see the little lass wearing the colour or ornament that her chosen lad admires. It is true that the "best girl" varies from week to week if not from day to day, but this special regard for a member of the opposite sex announces the dawn of a simple sentiment that will, a few years later, blossom out into the real passion which may fix a life's destiny.

The mental and moral changes that occur during the early years of adolescence call for help and sympathy of an even higher order than do the changes in physical structure and function. Some of these changes, such as shyness and reticence, may be the cause of considerable suffering to the girl and a perplexity to her elders, but on the whole they are comparatively easy of comprehension, and are more likely to elicit sympathy and kindness than blame. It is far otherwise with such changes as unseemly laughter, rough manners, and a nameless difference in the girl's manner when in the presence of the other sex. A girl who is usually quiet, modest, and sensible in her behaviour may suddenly become boisterous and self-asserting, there is a great deal of giggling, and altogether a disagreeable transformation which too frequently involves the girl in trouble with her mother or other guardian, and is very frequently harshly judged by the child herself. In proportion as self-discipline has been taught and self-control acquired, these outward manifestations are less marked, but in the case of the great majority of girls there are, at any rate, impulses having their origin in the yet immature and misunderstood sex impulse which cause the young woman herself annoyance and worry although she is as far from understanding their origin as her elders may be. The remedies for these troubles are various. First in order of time and in importance comes a habit of self-control and self-discipline that ought to be coeval with conscious life. Fathers and mothers are themselves to blame if their girl lapses from good behaviour when they have not inculcated ideals of obedience, duty, and self-discipline from babyhood. It seems such a little thing to let the child have its run of the cake-basket and the sweet-box; it is in the eyes of many parents so unimportant whether the little one goes to bed at the appointed time or ten minutes later; they argue that it can make no difference to her welfare in life or to her eternal destiny whether her obedience is prompt and cheerful or grudging and imperfect. One might as well argue that the proper planting of a seed, its regular watering, and the influences of sun and wind make no difference to the life of a tree. We have to bear carefully in mind that those who sow an act reap a habit, who sow a habit reap a character, who sow a character reap a destiny both in this world and in that which is eternal. It is mere selfishness, unconscious, no doubt, but none the less fatal, when parents to suit their own convenience omit to inculcate obedience, self-restraint, habits of order and unselfishness in their children. Youth is the time when the soul is apt to be shaken by sorrow's power and when stormy passions rage. The tiny rill starting from the mountainside can be readily deflected east or west, but the majestic river hastening to the sea is beyond all such arbitrary directions. So it is with the human being: the character and habit are directed easily in infancy, with difficulty during childhood, but they are well-nigh impossible of direction by the time adolescence is established. Those fathers and mothers who desire to have happiness and peace in connection with their adolescent boys and girls must take the trouble to direct them aright during the plastic years of infancy and childhood. All natural instincts implanted in us by Him who knew what was in the heart of man are in themselves right and good, but the exercise of these instincts may be entirely wrong in time or in degree. The sexual instinct, the affinity of boy to girl, the love of adult man and woman, are right and holy when exercised aright, and it is the result of "spoiling" when these good and noble instincts are wrongly exercised. All who love their country, all who love their fellow men, and all who desire that the kingdom of God should come, must surely do everything that is in their power to awaken the fathers and mothers of the land to a sense of their heavy responsibility and of their high privilege. In this we are entirely separated from and higher than the rest of the animal creation, in that on us lies the duty not only of calling into life a new generation of human beings, but also the still higher duty, the still greater privilege and the wider responsibility of bringing up those children to be themselves the worthy parents of the future, the supporters of their country's dignity, and joyful citizens of the household of God.

Another characteristic of adolescence is to be found in gregariousness, or what has been sometimes called the gang spirit. Boys, and to almost as great a degree girls, form themselves into companies or gangs, which frequently possess a high degree of organisation. They elaborate special languages, they have their own form of shorthand, their passwords, their rites and ceremonies. The gang has its elected leader, its officers, its members; and although it is liable to sudden disruption and seldom outlasts a few terms of school-life, each succeeding club or company is for the time being of paramount importance in the estimation of its members. The gang spirit may at times cause trouble and lead to anxiety, but if rightly directed it may be turned to good account. It is the germ of the future capacity to organise men and women into corporate life—the very method by which much public and national work is readily accomplished, but which is impossible to accomplish by individual effort.

3. Changes in the Religion of the Adolescent.—The religion of the adolescent is apt to be marked by fervour and earnest conviction, the phenomenon of "conversion" almost constantly occurring during adolescence. The girl looks upon eternal truths from a completely new standpoint, or at any rate with eyes that have been purged and illuminated by the throes of conversion. From a period of great anxiety and doubt she emerges to a time of intense love and devotion, to an eager desire to prove herself worthy, and to offer a sacrifice of the best powers she possesses. Unfortunately for peace of mind, the happy epoch succeeding conversion not unfrequently ends in a dismal time of intellectual doubt and spiritual darkness. Just as the embryonic love of the youthful adolescent leads to a time when the opposite sex is rather an object of dislike than of attraction, so the fervour of early conversion is apt to lead to a time of desolation; but just as the incomplete sex love of early adolescence finds its antitype and fine flower in the later fully developed love of honourable man and woman, so does the too rapturous and uncalculating religious devotion of these early years revive after the period of doubt, transfigured and glorified into the religious conviction and devotion which makes the strength, the joy, and the guiding principle of adult life.

Much depends on the circumstances and people surrounding the adolescent. Her unbounded capacity for hero-worship leads in many instances to a conscious or unconscious copying of parent, guardian, or teacher; and although the ideals of the young are apt to far outpace those of the adult whose days of illusion are over, yet they are probably formed on the same type. One sees this illustrated by generations in the same family holding much the same religious or political opinions and showing the same aptitude for certain professions, games, and pursuits. Much there is in heredity, but probably there is still more in environment.

CHAPTER II.
OUR DUTIES TOWARDS ADOLESCENT GIRLS.

These may be briefly summed up by saying that we have to provide adolescent girls with all things that are necessary for their souls and their bodies, but any such bald and wholesale enunciation of our duty helps but little in clearing one's ideas and in pointing out the actual manner in which we are to perform it.

First, with regard to the bodies of adolescent girls; Their primary needs, just like the primary needs of all living beings, are food, warmth, shelter, exercise and rest, with special care in sickness.

Food.—In spite of the great advance of knowledge in the present day, it is doubtful whether much practical advance has been made in the dietetics of children and adolescents, and it is to be feared that our great schools are especially deficient in this most important respect. Even when the age of childhood is past, young people require a much larger amount of milk than is usually included in their diet sheet. It would be well for them to begin the day with porridge and milk or some such cereal preparation. Coffee or cocoa made with milk should certainly have the preference over tea for breakfast, and in addition to the porridge or other such dish, fish, egg, or bacon, with plenty of bread and butter, should form the morning repast. The midday meal should consist of fresh meat, fish, or poultry, with an abundance of green vegetables and a liberal helping of sweet pudding. The articles of diet which are most deficient in our lists are milk, butter, and sugar. There is an old prejudice against sugar which is quite unfounded so far as the healthy individual is concerned. Cane sugar has recently been proved to be a most valuable muscle food, and when taken in the proper way for sweetening beverages, fruit, and puddings, it is entirely good. The afternoon meal should consist chiefly of bread and butter and milk or cocoa, with a fair proportion of simple, well-made cake, and in the case where animal food has been taken both at breakfast and dinner, the evening meal might well be bread and butter, bread and milk, or milk pudding with stewed or fresh fruit. But it is different in the case of those adolescents whose midday meal is necessarily slight, and who ought to have a thoroughly good dinner or supper early in the evening;

One would have thought it unnecessary to mention alcohol in speaking of the dietary of young people were it not that, strange to say, beer is still given at some of our public schools. It is extraordinary that wise and intelligent people should still give beer to young boys and girls at the very time when what they want is strength and not stimulus, food for the growing frame and nothing to stimulate the already exuberant passions.

An invariable rule with regard to the food of children should be that their meals should be regular, that they should consist of good, varied, nourishing food taken at regular hours, and that nothing should be eaten between meals. The practice of eating biscuits, fruit, and sweets between meals during childhood and adolescence not only spoils the digestion and impairs the nutrition at the time, but it is apt to lay the foundation of a constant craving for something which is only too likely to take the form of alcoholic craving in later years. It is impossible for the stomach to perform its duty satisfactorily if it is never allowed rest, and the introduction of stray morsels of food at irregular times prevents this, and introduces confusion into the digestive work, because there will be in the stomach at the same time food in various stages of digestion.

Warmth.—Warmth is one of the influences essential to health and to sound development, and although artificial warmth is more urgently required by little children and by old people than it is by young adults, still, if their bodies are to come to their utmost possible perfection, they require suitable conditions of temperature. This is provided in the winter partly by artificial heating of houses and partly by the wearing of suitable clothing. Ideal clothing is loose of texture and woven of wool, although a fairly good substitute can be obtained in materials that are made from cotton treated specially.

This is not the time or place in which to insist on the very grave dangers that accompany the use of ordinary flannelette, but a caution must be addressed in passing to those who provide clothing for others. In providing clothes it is necessary to remember the two reasons for their existence: (1) to cover the body, and (2) as far as possible to protect a large area of its surface against undue damp and cold.

Adolescents, as a rule, begin early to take a great interest in their clothes. From the time that the appreciation of the opposite sex commences, the child who has hitherto been indifferent or even slovenly in the matter of clothing takes a very living interest in it; indeed the adornment of person and the minute care devoted to details of the toilet by young people of both sexes remind one irresistibly of the preening of the feathers, the strutting and other antics of birds before their mates.

Girls especially are apt to forget the primary object of clothing, and to think of it too much as a means of adornment. This leads to excesses and follies such as tight waists, high-heeled shoes, to the ungainly crinoline or to indecent scantiness of skirts. Direct interference in these matters is badly tolerated, but much may be accomplished both by example and by cultivating a refined and artistic taste in sumptuary matters.

Sleep.—Amongst the most important of the factors that conduce to well-being both of body and mind must be reckoned an adequate amount of sleep. This has been made the subject of careful inquiry by Dr. Dukes of Rugby and Miss Alice Ravenhill. Both these trained and careful observers agree that the majority of young people get far too little rest and sleep. We have to remember that although fully-grown adults will take rest when they can get it in the daytime, young people are too active, and sometimes too restless, to give any repose to brain or muscle except during sleep. In the early years of adolescence ten hours sleep is none too much; even an adult in full work ought to have eight hours, and still more is necessary for the rapidly-growing, continually-developing, and never-resting adolescent. It is unfortunately a fact that even in the boarding schools of the well-to-do the provision of sleep is too limited, and for the children of the poor, whose homes are far from comfortable and who are accustomed to doing pretty nearly as their elders do, the night seldom begins before eleven or even twelve o'clock. It is one of the saddest sights of London to see small children dancing on the pavement in front of the public-houses up to a very late hour, while groups of loafing boys and hoydenish girls stand about at the street corners half the night. There is little wonder that the morning finds them heavy and unrefreshed, and that schoolwork suffers severely from want of the alert and vigorous attention that might be secured by a proper night's sleep.

Great harm is done by allowing children to take work home with them from school; if possible, the day's work should finish with school hours, and the scanty leisure should be spent in healthy exercise or in sleep.

Overcrowding.—In considering the question of adequate sleep it would be well to think of the conditions of healthy sleep.

For sleep to be refreshing and health-giving, the sleeper ought to have a comfortable bed and an abundant supply of fresh air. Unfortunately the great majority of our people both in town and country do not enjoy these advantages. In both town and country there is a great deficiency of suitable dwellings at rents that can be paid with the usual rate of wages. In consequence families are crowded into one, two, or three rooms, and even in the case of people far above the status of day labourers and artisans it is the exception and not the rule for each individual to have a separate bed. The question of ventilation is certainly better understood than it was a few years ago, but still leaves much to be desired, and there is still an urgent necessity for preaching the gospel of the open window.

Exercise.—In considering the question of the exercise of adolescents, one's thoughts immediately turn to athletics, games, and dancing. As a nation the English have always been fond of athletics, and have attributed to the influence of such team games as cricket and football not only their success in various competitions but also their success in the sterner warfare of life. This success has been obtained on the tented field and in the work of exploring, mountaineering, and other pursuits that make great demand not only on nerve and muscle but also on strength of character and powers of endurance.

Team games appear to be the especial property of adolescents, for young children are more or less individualistic and solitary in many of their games, but boys and girls alike prefer team games from the pre-adolescent age up to adult life. It is certain that no form of exercise is superior to these games: they call into play every muscle of the body, they make great demands on accuracy of eye and coordination, they also stimulate and develop habits of command, obedience, loyalty, and esprit de corps. In the great public schools of England, and in the private schools which look up to them as their models, team games are played, as one might say, in a religious spirit. The boy or girl who attempts to take an unfair advantage, or who habitually plays for his or her own hand, is quickly made to feel a pariah and an outcast. Among the greatest blessings that are conveyed to the children of the poorer classes is the instruction not only in the technique of team games but also in the inoculation of the spirit in which they ought to be played. It is absolutely necessary that the highest ideals connected with games should be handed down, for thus the children who perhaps do not always have the highest ideals before them in real life may learn through this mimic warfare how the battle of life must be fought and what are the characters of mind and body that deserve and ensure success. It has been well said that those who make the songs of a nation help largely to make its character, and equally surely those who teach and control the games of the adolescents are making or marring a national destiny.

Among the means of physical and moral advancement may be claimed gymnastics. And here, alas, this nation can by no means claim to be facile princeps. Not only have we been relatively slow in adopting properly systematised exercises, but even to the present day the majority of elementary schools are without properly fitted gymnasia and duly qualified teachers. The small and relatively poor Scandinavian nations have admirably fitted gymnasia in connection with their Folkschule, which correspond to our elementary schools. The exercises are based on those systematised by Ling; each series is varied, and is therefore the more interesting, and each lesson commences with simple, easily performed movements, leading on to those that are more elaborate and fatiguing, and finally passing through a descending series to the condition of repose.

The gymnasia where such exercises are taught in England are relatively few and far between, and it is lamentable to find that many excellent and well-appointed schools for children, whose parents pay large sums of money for their education, have no properly equipped gymnasia nor adequately trained teachers. When the question is put, "How often do you have gymnastics at your school?" the answer is frequently, "We have none," or, "Half an hour once a week." Exercises such as Ling's not only exercise every muscle in the body in a scientific and well-regulated fashion, but being performed by a number of pupils at once in obedience to words of command, discipline, co-operation, obedience to teachers, and loyalty to comrades, are taught at the same time. The deepest interest attaches to many of the more complex exercises, while some of them make large demands on the courage and endurance of the young people.

In Scandinavia the State provides knickerbockers, tunics, and gymnasium shoes for those children whose parents are too poor to provide them; and again, in Scandinavia there is very frequently the provision of bathrooms in which the pupils can have a shower bath and rub-down after the exercises. These bathrooms in connection with the gymnasia need not necessarily be costly; indeed many of them in Stockholm and Denmark merely consist of troughs in the cement floor, on the edge of which the children sit in a row while they receive a shower bath over their heads and bodies. The feet get well washed in the trough, and the smart douche of water on head and shoulders acts as an admirable tonic.

Another exercise which ought to be specially dear to a nation of islanders is swimming, and this, again, is a relatively cheap luxury too much neglected amongst us. Certainly there are public baths, but there are not enough to permit of all the elementary school children bathing even once a week, and still less have they the opportunity of learning to swim. There is much to be done yet before we can be justly proud of our national system of education. We must not lose sight of the ideal with which we started—viz. that we should endeavour to do the best that is possible for our young people in body, soul, and spirit. The three parts of our nature are intertwined, and a duty performed to one part has an effect on the whole.

CHAPTER III.
CARE OF THE ADOLESCENT GIRL IN SICKNESS.

If measured by the death-rate the period of adolescence should cause us little anxiety, but a careful examination into the state of health of children of school age shows us that it is a time in which disorders of health abound, and that although these disorders are not necessarily, nor even generally, fatal, they are frequent, they spoil the child's health, and inevitably bear fruit in the shape of an injurious effect on health in after life.

That the health of adolescents should be unstable is what we ought to expect from the general instability of the organism due to the rapidity of growth and the remarkable developmental changes that are crowded into these few years. Rapidity of growth and increase of weight are very generally recognised, although their effects upon health are apt to be overlooked. On the other hand, the still more remarkable development that occurs in adolescence is very generally ignored.

As a general rule the infectious fevers, the so-called childish diseases—such as measles, chicken-pox, and whooping-cough—are less common in adolescence than they are in childhood, while the special diseases of internal organs due to their overwork, or to their natural tendency to degeneration, is yet far in the future. The chief troubles of adolescents appear to be due to overstress which accompanies rapid development, to the difficulty of the whole organism in adapting itself to new functions and altered conditions, and no doubt in some measure to the unwisdom both of the young people and of their advisers.

This is not the place for a general treatise on the diseases of adolescents, but a few of the commonest and most obvious troubles should be noted.

The Teeth.—It is quite surprising to learn what a very large percentage of young soldiers are refused enlistment in the army on account of decayed or defective teeth, and anyone who has examined the young women candidates for the Civil Service and for Missionary Societies must have recognised that their teeth are in no way better than those of the young men. In addition to several vacancies in the dental series, it is by no means unusual to find that a candidate has three or even five teeth severely decayed. The extraordinary thing is that not only the young people and their parents very generally fail to recognise the gravity of this condition, but that even their medical advisers have frequently acquiesced in a state of things that is not only disagreeable but dangerous. A considerable proportion of people with decayed teeth have also suppuration about the margins of the gums and around the roots of the teeth. This pyorrhoea alveolaris, as it is called, constitutes a very great danger to the patient's health, the purulent discharge teems with poisonous micro-organisms, which being constantly swallowed are apt to give rise to septic disease in various organs. It is quite probable that some cases of gastric ulcer are due to this condition, so too are some cases of appendicitis, it has been known to cause a peculiarly fatal form of heart disease, and it is also responsible for the painful swelling of the joints of the fingers, with wasting of the muscles and general weakness which goes by the name of rheumatoid arthritis. In addition to this there are many local affections, such as swollen glands in the neck, that may be due to this poisonous discharge. One would think that the mere knowledge that decayed teeth can cause all this havoc would lead to a grand rush to the dentist, but so far from being the case, doctors find it extremely difficult to induce their patients to part with this unsightly, evil-smelling, and dangerous decayed tooth.

The Throat.—Some throat affections, such as diphtheria and quinsy, are well known and justly dreaded; and although many a child's life has been sacrificed to the slowness of its guardians to procure medical advice and the health-restoring antitoxin, yet on the whole the public conscience is awake to this duty. Far otherwise is it with chronic diseases of the tonsils: they may be riddled with small cysts, they may be constantly in a condition of subacute inflammation dependent on a septic condition, but no notice is taken except when chill, constipation, or a general run-down state of health aggravates the chronic into a temporary acute trouble. And yet it is perhaps not going too far to say that for one young girl who is killed or invalided rapidly by diphtheria there are hundreds who are condemned to a quasi-invalid life owing to this persistent supply of poison to the system.

Another condition of the throat which causes much ill-health is well known to the public under the name of adenoids. Unfortunately, however, many people have an erroneous idea that children will "grow out of adenoids." Even if this were true it is extremely unwise to wait for so desirable an event. Adenoids may continue to grow, and during the years that they are present they work great mischief. Owing to the blocking of the air-passages the mouth is kept constantly open, greatly to the detriment of the throat and lungs. Owing to the interference with the circulation at the back of the nose and throat, a considerable amount both of apparent and real stupidity is produced, the brain works less well than it ought, and the child's appearance is ruined by the flat, broad bridge of the nose and the gaping mouth. The tale of troubles due to adenoids is not even yet exhausted; a considerable amount of discharge collects about them which it is not easy to clear away, it undergoes very undesirable changes, and is then swallowed to the great detriment of the stomach and the digestion. The removal of septic tonsils and of adenoids is most urgently necessary, and usually involves little distress or danger. The change in the child's health and appearance that can thus be secured is truly wonderful, especially if it be taught, as it should be, to keep its mouth shut and to breathe through the nose. In the course of a few months the complexion will have cleared, the expression will have regained its natural intelligence, digestion will be well performed, and the child's whole condition will be that of alert vigour instead of one of listless and sullen indifference.

Errors of Digestion.—From the consideration of certain states of the nose, mouth, and throat, it is easy to turn to what is so often their consequence. Many forms of indigestion are due to the septic materials swallowed. It would not, however, be fair to say that all indigestion is thus caused; not infrequently indigestion is due to errors of diet, and here the blame must be divided between the poverty and ignorance of many parents and the self-will of adolescents. The foods that are best for young people—such as bread, milk, butter, sugar, and eggs—are too frequently scarce in their dietaries owing to their cost; and again, in the case of many girls whose parents are able and willing to provide them with a thoroughly satisfactory diet-sheet, dyspepsia is caused by their refusal to take what is good for them, and by their preference for unsuitable and indigestible viands.

A further cause of indigestion must be sought in the haste with which food is too often eaten. The failure to rise at the appointed time leads to a hasty breakfast, and this must eventually cause indigestion. The food imperfectly masticated and not sufficiently mixed with saliva enters the stomach ill-prepared, and the hasty rush to morning school or morning work effectually prevents the stomach from dealing satisfactorily with the mass so hastily thrust into it.

There is an old saying that "Those whom the gods will destroy they first make mad," and in many instances young people who fall victims to the demon of dyspepsia owe their sorrows, if not to madness, at any rate to ignorance and want of consideration. The defective teeth, septic tonsils, discharging adenoids, poverty of their parents and their own laziness, all conspire to cause digestive troubles which bear a fruitful crop of further evils, for thus are caused such illnesses as anæmia and gastric ulcer.

Constipation claims a few words to itself. And here again we ought to consider certain septic processes. The refuse of the food should travel along the bowels at a certain rate, but if owing to sluggishness of their movements or to defects in the quality and amount of their secretion, the refuse is too long retained the masses become unduly dry, and, constantly shrinking in volume, are no longer capable of being urged along the tube at the proper rate. In consequence of this the natural micro-organisms of the intestine cease to be innocent and become troublesome; they lead in the long run to a peculiar form of blood-poisoning, and to so many diseased conditions that it is impossible to deal with them at the present moment. The existence of constipation is too often a signal for the administration of many doses of medicine. The wiser, the less harmful, and the more effectual method of dealing with it would be to endeavour to secure the natural action of the bowels by a change in the diet, which should contain more vegetable and less animal constituents. The patient should also be instructed to drink plenty of water, either hot or cold, a large glassful on going to bed and one on first awaking, and also if necessary an hour before each meal. Steady exercise is also of very great service, and instead of starting so late as to have no time for walking to school or work, a certain portion of the daily journey should be done on foot. Further, in all cases where it is possible, team games, gymnastics, and dancing should be called in to supplement the walk.

Headache.—Headache may be due to so many different causes that it would be impossible in this little book to adequately consider them, but it would not be fair to omit to mention that in many cases the headache of young people is due to their want of spectacles. The idea that spectacles are only required by people advanced in life is by this time much shaken, but even now not only many parents object to their children enjoying this most necessary assistance to imperfect vision, but also employers may be found so foolish and selfish as to refuse to employ those persons who need to wear glasses. The folly as well as selfishness of this objection is demonstrated by the far better work done by a person whose vision has been corrected, and the absolute danger incurred by all who have to deal with machinery if vision is imperfect. Among other causes for headache are the defects of mouth, throat, stomach, and bowels already described, because in all of them there is a supply of septic material to the blood which naturally causes headache and other serious symptoms.

Abnormalities of Menstruation.—The normal period should occur at regular intervals about once a month. Its duration and amount vary within wide limits, but in each girl it should remain true to her individual type, and it ought not to be accompanied by pain or distress. As a rule the period starts quite normally, and it is not until the girl's health has been spoiled by over-exertion of body or mind, by unwise exertion during the period, or by continued exposure to damp or cold, that it becomes painful and abnormal in time or in amount.

One of the earliest signs of approaching illness—such as consumption, anæmia, and mental disorder—is to be found in the more or less sudden cessation of the period. This should always be taken as a danger-signal, and as indicating the need of special medical advice.

Another point that should enter into intimate talk with girls is to make them understand the co-relation of their own functions to the great destiny that is in store. A girl is apt to be both shocked and humiliated when she first hears of menstruation and its phenomena. Should this function commence before she is told about it, she will necessarily look upon it with disgust and perhaps with fear. It is indeed a most alarming incident in the case of a girl who knows nothing about it, but if, before the advent of menstruation, it be explained to her that it is a sign of changes within her body that will gradually, after the lapse of some years, fit her also to take her place amongst the mothers of the land, her shame and fear will be converted into modest gladness, and she will readily understand why she is under certain restrictions, and has at times to give up work or pleasure in order that her development may be without pain, healthy, and complete.

CHAPTER IV.
MENTAL AND MORAL TRAINING.

The years of adolescence, during which rapid growth and development inevitably cause so much stress and frequently give rise to danger, are the very years in which the weight of school education necessarily falls most heavily. The children of the poor leave school at fourteen years of age, just the time when the children of the wealthier classes are beginning to understand the necessity of education and to work with a clearer realisation of the value and aim of lessons. The whole system of education has altered of late years, and school work is now conducted far more intelligently and with a greater appreciation of the needs and capacities of the pupils than it was some fifty years ago. Work is made more interesting, the relation of different studies to each other is more adequately put in evidence, and the influence that school studies have on success in after life is more fully realised by all concerned. The system of training is, however, far from perfect. In the case of girls, more particularly, great care has to be exercised not to attempt to teach too much, and to give careful consideration to the physiological peculiarities of the pupils. It is impossible for girls who are undergoing such rapid physiological and psychical changes to be always equally able and fit for strenuous work. There are days in every girl's life when she is not capable of her best work, and when a wise and sympathetic teacher will see that it is better for her to do comparatively little. And yet these slack times are just those in which there is the greatest danger of a girl indulging in daydreams, and when her thoughts need to be more than usually under control. These times may be utilised for lighter subjects and for such manual work as does not need great physical exertion. It is not a good time for exercises, for games, for dancing, and for gardening, nor are they the days on which mathematics should be pressed, but they are days in which much supervision is needed, and when time should not be permitted to hang heavily on hand.

Just as there are days in which consideration should be shown, so too there are longer periods of time in which it is unwise for a girl to be pressed to prepare for or to undergo a strenuous examination. The brain of the girl appears to be as good as that of the boy, while her application, industry, and emulation are far in advance of his, but she has these physiological peculiarities, and if they are disregarded there will not only be an occasional disastrous failure in bodily or mental health, but girls as a class will fail to do the best work of which they are capable, and will fail to reap the fullest advantage from an education which is costly in money, time, and strength. It follows that the curriculum for girls presents greater difficulties than the curriculum for boys, and that those ladies who are responsible for the organisation of a school for girls need to be women of great resource, great patience, and endowed with much sympathetic insight. The adolescent girl will generally do little to help her teachers in this matter. She is incapable of recognising her own limitations, she is full of emulation, and is desirous of attaining and keeping a good position not only in her school but also in the University or in any other public body for whose examination she may present herself. The young girl most emphatically needs to be saved from herself, and she has to learn the lessons of obedience and of cheerful acquiescence in restrictions that certainly appear to her simply vexatious.

One of the difficulties in private schools arises from the necessity of providing occupation for every hour of the waking day, while avoiding the danger of overwork with its accompanying exhaustion. In the solution of this problem such subjects as gymnastics, games, dancing, needlework, cooking, and domestic economy will come in as a welcome relief from the more directly intellectual studies, and equally as a relief to the conscientious but hard-pressed woman who is trying to save her pupils from the evils of unoccupied time on the one hand and undue mental pressure on the other.

Boys, and to a less extent girls, attending elementary schools who leave at fourteen are not likely to suffer in the same way or from the same causes. One of the difficulties in their case is that they leave school just when work is becoming interesting and before habits of study have been formed, indeed before the subjects taught have been thoroughly assimilated, and that therefore in the course of a few years little may be left of their painfully acquired and too scanty knowledge. Free education has been given to the children of the poor for nearly fifty years, and yet the mothers who were schoolgirls in the seventies and eighties appear to have saved but little from the wreck of their knowledge except the power to sign their names and to read in an imperfect and blundering manner.

Here, too, there are many problems to be solved, one among them being the great necessity of endeavouring to correlate the lessons given in school to the work that the individual will have to perform in after life. It would appear as if the girls of the elementary schools, in addition to reading, writing, and simple arithmetic, sufficient to enable them to write letters, to read books, and to keep simple household accounts, ought to be taught the rudiments of cookery, the cutting out and making of garments, and the best methods of cleansing as applied to houses, household utensils and clothing. In addition, and as serious subjects, not merely as a recreation, they should be taught gymnastics, part singing and mother-craft. No doubt in individual schools much of this modification of the curriculum has been accomplished, but more remains to be done before we can be satisfied that we have done the best in our power to fit the children of the country for their life's work.

Another of the great problems connected with the children in elementary schools, a problem which, indeed, arises out of their leaving at fourteen, is that of the Continuation School or Evening School, and the system which is known as "half-timing." It is well known that although young people from fourteen to sixteen years of age are well able to profit by continued instruction, they are, with very few exceptions, not at all well adapted for commencing their life's work as industrials. The general incoherency and restlessness peculiar to that age frequently lead to a change of employment every few months, while their general irresponsibility and want of self-control lead to frequent disputes with foremen and other officials in factories and shops, in consequence of which the unfortunate child is constantly out of work. In proportion to the joy and pride caused by the realised capacity to earn money and by the sense of independence that employment brings, is the unhappiness, and in many cases the misery, due to unemployment, and to repeated failures to obtain and to keep an independent position. The boy or girl out of work has an uneasy feeling that he or she has not earned the just and expected share towards household expenses. The feeling of dependence and well-nigh of disgrace causes a rapid deterioration in health and spirits, and it is only too likely that in many instances where unemployment is continuous or frequently repeated, the unemployed will quickly become the unemployable.

So far as the young people themselves are concerned, it would be nearly always an unmixed benefit that they should pass at fourteen into a Technical School or Continuation School, as the case may be. Among the great difficulties to the solution of this problem is the fact that in many working-class households the few weekly shillings brought into the family store by the elder children are of very real importance, and although the raising of the age of possible employment and independence would enable the next generation to work better and to earn higher and more continuous wages, it is difficult for the parents to acquiesce in the present deprivation involved, even though it represents so much clear gain in the not distant future.

At the present time there are Evening Schools, but this system does not work well. All busy people are well aware that after a hard day's work neither brain nor body is in the best possible condition for two or three hours of serious mental effort. The child who has spent the day in factory or shop has really pretty nearly used up all his or her available mental energy, and after the evening meal is naturally heavy, stupid, irritable, and altogether in a bad condition for further effort. The evenings ought to be reserved for recreation, for the gymnasium, the singing class, the swimming bath, and even for the concert and the theatre.

The system of "half-timing" during ordinary school life does not work well, and it would be a great pity should a similar system be introduced in the hope of furthering the education of boys and girls who are just entering industrial life. There is reason to hope that a great improvement in education will be secured by Mr. Hayes Fisher's bill.

Another subject to which the attention of patriots and philanthropists ought to be turned is the sort of employment open to children at school-leaving age. The greatest care should be taken to diminish the number of those who endeavour to achieve quasi-independence in those occupations which are well known as "blind alleys." In England it is rare that girls should seek these employments, but in Scotland there is far too large a number of girl messengers. In this particular, the case of the girl is superior to that of the boy. The "tweeny" develops into housemaid or cook; the young girls employed in superior shops to wait on the elder shopwomen hope to develop into their successors, and the girls who nurse babies on the doorsteps are, after all, acquiring knowledge and dexterity that may fit them for domestic service or for the management of their own families a few years later.

The girls of the richer classes have not the same difficulties as their poorer sisters. They generally remain at school until a much later age, and subsequently have the joy and stimulus of college life, of foreign travel, of social engagements, or of philanthropic enterprise. Still, a residue remains even of girls of this class whose own inclinations, or whose family circumstances, lead to an aimless, purposeless existence, productive of much injury to both body and mind, and only too likely to end in hopeless ennui and nervous troubles. It should be thoroughly understood by parents and guardians that no matter what the girl's circumstances may be, she ought always to have an abundance of employment. The ideas of obligation and of duty should not be discarded when school and college life cease. The well-to-do girl should be encouraged to take up some definite employment which would fill her life and provide her with interests and duties. Any other arrangement tends to make the time between leaving school or college and a possible marriage not only a wasted time but also a seed-time during which a crop is sown of bad habits, laziness of body, and slackness of mind, that subsequently bear bitter fruit. It is quite time for us to recognise that unemployment and absence of duties is as great a disadvantage to the rich as it is to the poor; the sort of employment must necessarily differ, but the spirit in which it is to be done is the same.

One point that one would wish to emphasise with regard to all adolescents is that although occupation for the whole day is most desirable, hard work should occupy but a certain proportion of the waking hours. For any adolescent, or indeed for any of us to attempt to work hard for twelve or fourteen hours out of the twenty-four is to store up trouble. It is not possible to lay down any hard and fast rule as to the length of hours of work, because the other factors in the problem vary so greatly. One person may be exhausted by four hours of intellectual effort, whereas another is less fatigued by eight; and further, the daily occupations vary greatly in the demand that they make on attention and on such qualities as reason, judgment, and power of initiation. Those who teach or learn such subjects as mathematics, or those who are engaged in such occupations as portrait-painting and the higher forms of musical effort, must necessarily take more out of themselves than those who are employed in feeding a machine, in nursing a baby, or in gardening operations.

CHAPTER V.
THE FINAL AIM OF EDUCATION.

The great problem before those who have the responsibility for the training of the young is that of preparing them to take their place in the world as fathers, mothers, and citizens, and among the fundamental duties connected with this responsibility must come the placing before the eyes of the young people high ideals, attractive examples, and the securing to them the means of adequate preparation. As a nation it seems to be with us at present as it was with the people of Israel in the days of Eli: "the word of the Lord was precious (or scarce) in those days; there was no open vision." We seem to have come to a time of civilisation in which there is much surface refinement and a widespread veneer of superficial knowledge, but in which there is little enthusiasm and in which the great aim and object of teaching and of training is but too little realised. In the endeavour to know a little of all things we seem to have lost the capacity for true and exhaustive knowledge of anything. It would appear as if the remedy for this most unsatisfactory state of things has to commence long before the years of adolescence, even while the child is yet in its cradle. The old-fashioned ideas of duty, obedience, and discipline must be once more household words and living entities before the race can enter on a period of regeneration. We want a poet with the logic of Browning, the sweetness of Tennyson, and the force of Rudyard Kipling, to sing a song that would penetrate through indifference, sloth, and love of pleasure, and make of us the nation that we might be, and of which the England of bygone years had the promise.

Speaking specially with regard to girls, let us first remember that the highest earthly ideal for a woman is that she should be a good wife and a good mother. It is not necessary to say this in direct words to every small girl, but she ought to be so educated, so guided, as to instinctively realise that wifehood and motherhood is the flower and perfection of her being. This is the hope and ideal that should sanctify her lessons and sweeten the right and proper discipline of life. All learning, all handicraft, and all artistic training should take their place as a preparation to this end. Each generation that comes on to the stage of life is the product of that which preceded it. It is the flower of the present national life and the seed of that which is to come. We ought to recognise that all educational aims and methods are really subordinate to this great end; if this were properly realised by adolescents it would be of the greatest service and help in their training. The deep primal instinct of fatherhood and motherhood would help them more than anything else to seek earnestly andsuccessfully for the highest attainable degree of perfection of their own bodies, their own minds, and their own souls. It is, however, impossible to aim at an ideal that is unseen and even unknown, and although the primal instinct exists in us all, its fruition is greatly hindered by the way in which it is steadily ignored, and by the fact that any proclamation of its existence is considered indiscreet and even indelicate. How are children to develop a holy reverence for their own bodies unless they know of their wonderful destiny? If they do not recognise that at least in one respect God has confided to them in some measure His own creative function, how can they jealously guard against all that would injure their bodies and spoil their hopes for the exercise of this function? There is, even at the present time, a division of opinion as to when and in what manner children are to be made aware of their august destiny. We are indeed only now beginning to realise that ignorance is not necessarily innocence, and that knowledge of these matters may be sanctified and blessed. It is, however, certain that the conspiracy of silence which lasted so many years has brought forth nothing but evil. If a girl remains ignorant of physiological facts, the shock of the eternal realities of life that come to her on marriage is always pernicious and sometimes disastrous. If, on the other hand, such knowledge is obtained from servants and depraved playfellows, her purity of mind must be smirched and injured.

Even among those who hold that children ought to be instructed, there is a division of opinion as to when this instruction is to begin. Some say at puberty, others a few years later, perhaps on the eve of marriage, and yet others think that the knowledge will come with less shock, with less personal application, and therefore in a more natural and useful manner from the very beginning of conscious life. These last would argue—why put the facts of reproduction on a different footing from those of digestion and respiration? As facts in the physical life they hold a precisely similar position. Upon the due performance of bodily functions depends the welfare of the whole organism, and although reproduction, unlike the functions of respiration and digestion, is not essential to the life of the individual, it is essential to the life of the nation.

The facts of physiology are best taught to little children by a perfectly simple recognition of the phenomena of life around them — the cat with her kittens, the bird with its fledgelings, and still more the mother with her infant, are all common facts and beautiful types of motherhood. Instead of inventing silly and untrue stories as to the origin of the kitten and the fledgeling, it is better and wiser to answer the child's question by a direct statement of fact, that God has given the power to His creatures to perpetuate themselves, that the gift of Life is one of His good gifts bestowed in mercy on all His creatures. The mother's share in this gift and duty can be observed by, and simply explained to, the child from its earliest years; it comes then with no shock, no sense of shame, but as a type of joy and gladness, an image of that holiest of all relations, the Eternal Mother and the Heavenly Child.

Somewhat later in life, probably immediately before puberty in boys and shortly after puberty in girls, the father's share in this mystery may naturally come up for explanation. The physiological facts connected with this are not so constantly in evidence before children, and therefore do not press for explanation in the same way as do those of motherhood, but the time comes soon in the schoolboy's life when the special care of his own body has to be urged on him, and this knowledge ought to come protected by the sanction that unless he is faithful to his trust he cannot look to the reward of a happy home life with wife and children. In the case of the girl the question as to fatherhood is more likely to arise out of the reading of the Bible or other literature, or by her realisation that at any rate in the case of human parenthood there is evidently the intermediation of a father. The details of this knowledge need not necessarily be pressed on the adolescent girl, but it is a positive cruelty to allow the young woman to marry without knowing the facts on which her happiness depends.

Another way in which the mystery of parenthood can be simply and comfortably taught is through the study of vegetable physiology. The fertilisation of the ovules by pollen which falls directly from the anthers on to the stigma can be used as a representation of similar facts in animal physiology. It is very desirable, however, that this study of the vegetable should succeed and not precede that of the domestic animals in the teaching of boys and girls.

Viewed from this standpoint there is surely no difficulty to the parent in imparting to the child this necessary knowledge. We have to remember that children have to know the mysteries of life. They cannot live in the world without seeing the great drama constantly displayed to them in family life and in the lives of domesticated animals. They cannot read the literature of Greece and Rome, nay, they cannot study the Book of Books, without these facts being constantly brought to mind. A child's thirst for the interpretation of this knowledge is imperative and unsatiable—not from prurience nor from evil-mindedness, but in obedience to a law of our nature, the child demands this knowledge—and will get it. It is for fathers and mothers to say whether these sublime and beautiful mysteries shall be lovingly and reverently unveiled by themselves or whether the child's mind shall be poisoned and all beauty and reverence destroyed by depraved school-fellows and vulgar companions.

In the hope of securing the purity, reverence and piety of our children, in the hope that they may grow up worthy of their high destiny, let us do what we may to keep their honour unsmirched, to preserve their innocence, and to lead them on from the unconscious goodness of childhood to the clear-eyed, fully conscious dignity of maturity, that our sons may grow up as young plants, and our daughters as the polished corners of the temple.

PART II.: BOYS.

CHAPTER I.

PREVALENCE OF IMPURITY AMONG BOYS: THE AUTHOR'S OWN EXPERIENCE.

Of the perils which beset the growing boy all are recognised, and, in a measure, guarded against except the most inevitable and most fatal peril of all. In all that concerns the use and abuse of the reproductive organs the great majority of boys have hitherto been left without adult guidance, and have imbibed their ideas from the coarser of their companions and from casual references to the subject in the Bible and other books. Under these conditions very few boys escape two of the worst dangers into which it is possible for a lad to fall—the artificial stimulation of the reproductive organs and the acquisition of degraded ideas on the subject of sex. That many lives are thus prematurely shortened, that many constitutions are permanently enfeebled, that very many lads who might otherwise have striven successfully against the sexual temptations of adult life succumb—almost without a struggle—to them, can be doubted by no one who is familiar with the inner life of boys and men.

Of these two evils, self-abuse, though productive of manifold and disastrous results, is distinctly the less. Many boys outgrow the physical injuries which, in ignorance, they inflict upon themselves in youth; but very few are able wholly to cleanse themselves from the foul desires associated in their minds with sex. These desires make young men impotent in the face of temptation. Under their evil dominance, even men of kind disposition will, by seduction, inflict on an innocent girl agony, misery, degradation, and premature death. They will indulge In the most degrading of all vices with prostitutes on the street. They will defile the atmosphere of social life with filthy talk and ribald jest. Even a clean and ennobling passion can do little to redeem them. The pure stream of human love is made turbid with lust. After a temporary uplifting in marriage the soul is again dragged down, marriage vows are broken and the blessings of home life are turned into wormwood and gall.

That a system so destructive of physical and of spiritual health should have lasted almost intact until now will, I believe, shortly become a matter for general amazement; for while evidence of the widespread character of youthful perversion is a product of quite recent years, the assumptions on which this system has been based are unreasonable and incapable of proof.

Since conclusive evidence of the prevalence of impurity among boys is available, I will not at present invite the reader to examine the assumptions which lead most people to a contrary belief. When I do so, I shall hope to demonstrate that we might reasonably expect to find things precisely as they are. In the first and second chapters we shall see to what conclusions teachers who have actual experience in the matter have been led.

There are several teachers whose authority in most matters stands so very much above my own that it might seem presumptuous to begin by laying my own experiences before the reader; but I venture to take this course because no other teacher, as far as I know, has published quite such definite evidence as I have done; and I think that the more general statements of such eminent men as Canon Lyttelton, Mr. A.C. Benson, and Dr. Clement Dukes will appeal to the reader more powerfully when he has some idea of the manner in which conclusions on this subject may be reached. I have some reason, also, for the belief that the paper I read in 1908 at the London University before the International Congress on Moral Education has been considered of great significance by very competent judges. By a special decision of the Executive of the Congress it—alone of all sectional papers—was printed in extenso in the official report. Later on, it came under the notice of Sir R. Baden-Powell, at whose request it was republished in the Headquarters Gazette—the official organ of the Boy Scout movement.

It certainly did require some courage at the time to put my results before the public, for I was not then aware that men of great eminence in the educational world had already made equally sweeping, if less definite, statements. Emboldened by this fact and by the commendations above referred to, I venture to quote the greater part of this short paper.

"The opinions I am about to put forward are based almost entirely on my own twenty years' experience as a housemaster. My house contains forty-eight boys, who vary in age from ten to nineteen and come from comfortable middle-class homes.

"Private interviews with individual boys in my study have been the chief vehicle of my teaching and the chief source of my information. My objects in these interviews have been to warn boys against the evils of private impurity, to supply them with a certain amount of knowledge on sexual subjects in order to prevent a prurient curiosity, and to induce them to confide to me the history of their own knowledge and difficulties. In my early days I interviewed those only who appeared to me to be obviously suffering from the effects of impurity, and, of late years, the extreme pressure of my work has forced me very reluctantly to recur to this plan.

"For several years, however, I was accustomed to interview every boy under my care during his first term with me. Very rarely have I failed in these interviews so to secure a boy's confidence as to learn the salient facts of the history of his inner life. Sunday afternoon addresses to the Sixth Form on the sexual dangers of late youth and early manhood have resulted at times in elder boys themselves seeking an interview with me. Such spontaneous confidences have naturally been fuller, and therefore more instructive, than the confidences I have invited.

"Many people are inclined to look upon the instruction of boys in relation to adolescence as needless and harmful; needless because few boys, they imagine, awake to the consciousness and problems of sex until manhood; harmful because the pristine innocence of the mind is, they think, destroyed, and evils are suggested of which a boy might otherwise remain unconscious. To one who knows what boys really are such ideas are nothing less than ludicrous.

"Boys come to our school from many different classes of preparatory and secondary schools. Almost every such school seems to possess a few boys who delight to initiate younger boys into sexual knowledge, and usually into knowledge of solitary vice. The very few boys who have come to me quite ignorant of these matters have come either straight from home at ten or eleven, or from a school in which a few young boys are educated with girls. Of boys who have come under my care as late as twelve I have known but two who even professed total ignorance on sexual subjects, and in one of these cases I am quite sure that no such ignorance existed.

"In a large majority of cases solitary vice has been learned and practised before a boy has got into his teens. The lack of insight parents display in relation to these questions is quite phenomenal. The few who mention the subject to me are always quite satisfied of the complete 'innocence' of their boys. Some of the most precocious and unclean boys I have known have been thus confidently commended to me. Boys are wholly unsuspicious of the extent to which their inner life lies open to the practised eye, and they feel secure that nothing can betray their secrets if they themselves do not.

"In no department of our life are George Eliot's words truer than in this department: 'Our daily familiar life is but a hiding of ourselves from each other behind a screen of trivial words and deeds, and those who sit with us at the same hearth are often the farthest off from the deep human soul within us—full of unspoken evil and unacted good.' We cannot prevent a boy's obtaining information on sexual questions. Our choice lies between leaving him to pick it up from unclean and vulgar minds, which will make it guilty and impure, and giving it ourselves in such a way as to invest it from the first with a sacred character.

"Another idea which my experience proves to be an entire delusion is the idea that a boy's natural refinement is a sufficient protection against defilement. Some of the most refined boys I have had the pleasure of caring for have been pronounced victims of solitary sin. That it is a sin at all, that it has, indeed, any significance, either ethical or spiritual, has not so much as occurred to most of them. On what great moral question dare we leave the young to find their own way absolutely without guidance? In this most difficult and dangerous of all questions we leave the young soul, stirred by novel and blind impulses, to grope in the darkness. Is it any wonder if it fails to see things in their true relations?

"Again, it is sometimes thought that the consequences of secret sin are so patent as to deter a boy from the sin itself. So far is this from being the case that I have never yet found a single boy (even among those who have, through it, made almost complete wrecks physically and mentally) who has of himself connected these consequences with the sin itself. I have, on the other hand, known many sad cases in which, through the weakening of will power, which this habit causes, boys of high ideals have fallen again and again after their eyes have been fully opened. This sin is rarely a conscious moral transgression. The boy is a victim to be sympathised with and helped, not an offender to be reproved and punished."

I desire to call the attention of the reader to two points in the foregoing extract. I was particular in giving my credentials to state the character and limitations of my experience. Everywhere in life one finds confident and sweeping generalisations made by men who have little or no experience to appeal to. This is specially the case in the educational world, and perhaps most of all in discussions on this very subject. Some men, at least, are willing to instruct the public with nothing better to guide them than the light of Nature. It would greatly assist the quest of truth if everyone who ventures to address the public on this question would first present his credentials.

There is danger lest the reader should discount the significance of the statements I make in the foregoing paper by falling into the error of supposing that the facts stated apply, after all, to one school only. This is not by any means so. The facts have been collected at one school; but those which refer to the prevalence of sex knowledge and of masturbation have reference solely to the condition of boys when they first entered, and are significant of the conditions which obtain at some scores of schools and in many homes. I venture here to quote and to warmly endorse Canon Lyttelton's opinion: "It is, however, so easy to be misunderstood in this matter that I must insert a caution against an inference which may be drawn from these words, viz. that school life is the origin of immorality among boys. The real origin is to be found in the common predisposition to vicious conceptions, which is the result of neglect. Nature provides in almost every case an active curiosity on this subject; and that curiosity must be somehow allayed; and if it were not allayed at school, false and depraved ideas would be picked up at home.... So readily does an ignorant mind at an early age take in teaching about these subjects that there are no conceivable conditions of modern social life not fraught with grave peril to a young boy, if once he has been allowed to face them quite unprepared, either by instruction or by warning. And this manifestly applies to life at home, or in a day-school, or in a boarding-school to an almost equal degree."

One of the facts which I always tried to elicit from boys was the source of their information, or rather the character of that source, for I was naturally anxious not to ask a boy to incriminate any individual known to me. In many cases, information came first to the boy athome from a brother, or cousin, or casual acquaintance, or domestic servant. In one of the worst cases I have known the information was given to a boy by another boy—an entire stranger to him—whom he happened to meet on a country road when cycling. Since boys meet one another very much more at school than elsewhere and spend three-fourths of their lives there, of course information is more often obtained at school than at home. My own experience leads me to think that in this respect the day-school—probably on account of its mixed social conditions—is worse than the boarding-school.

Before passing from matters of personal experience, it may interest the reader if I give particulars of a few typical cases to illustrate some points on which I have insisted.

Case A.—The father and mother of a boy close on thirteen came to see me before entering the lad. They had no idea that I was specially interested in purity-teaching; but they were anxious to ascertain what precautions we took against the corruption of small boys. They struck me as very good parents. I was specially pleased that they were alive to the dangers of impurity, and that the mother could advert openly to the matter without embarrassment. I advised them to give the boy explicit warning; but they said that they were anxious to preserve his innocence as long as possible. He was at present absolutely simple, and they hoped that he would long remain so. It was a comfort to them that I was interested in the subject, and they would leave the boy with confidence in my care. As soon as I saw the boy, I found it difficult to believe in his innocence; and I soon discovered that he was thoroughly corrupt. Not merely did he begin almost at once to corrupt other boys, but he actually gave them his views on brothels! In a private interview with me he admitted all this, and told me that he was corrupted at ten years of age, when he was sent, after convalescence from scarlet fever, to a country village for three months. There he seems to have associated with a group of street boys, who gave him such information as they had, and initiated him into self-abuse. Since then he had been greedily seeking further information and passing it on.

Case B. — A delicate, gentle boy of eleven, an only son, was sent to me by an intellectual father, who had been his constant companion. The lad was very amiable and well-intentioned. A year later he gave me particulars of his corruption by a cousin, who was three years older than he. Since that time — particularly of late — he had practised masturbation. He had not the least idea that it was hurtful or evenunrefined, and thought that it was peculiar to himself and his cousin. He knew from his cousin the chief facts of maternity and paternity, but had not spoken to other boys about them. He was intensely anxious to cleanse himself entirely, and promised to let me know of any lapse, should it occur. In the following vacation he developed pneumonia. For some days his life hung in the balance, and then flickered out. His father wrote me a letter of noble resignation. Terribly as he felt his loss, he was greatly consoled, he said, by the knowledge that his boy had died while his mind was innocent and before he could know even what temptation was. It is needless to add that I never hinted the real facts to the father; and — without altering any material detail — I am disguising the case lest it should possibly be recognised by him. I have often wondered whether, when the lad's life hung in the balance, it might not have been saved if Death's scale had not been weighted by the child's lowered vitality.

Case C. — A boy of fourteen came to me. He was a miserable specimen in every way — pale, lethargic, stupid almost beyond belief. He had no mother; and the father, though a man of leisure, evidently found it difficult to make the lad much of a companion. I felt certain from the first that the boy was an exceptionally bad victim of self-abuse; And this I told his father, advising him to investigate the matter. He was horrified at my diagnosis, and committed the great indiscretion of taxing the boy with self-abuse as though it were a conscious andgrave fault. The father wrote during the vacation saying that he found I was entirely mistaken: not, content with the lad's assurance, he had watched him with the utmost care. As soon as the boy returned to school I interviewed him. He admitted readily that he had long masturbated himself daily—sometimes oftener. He had first—as far as he could remember, at about six—had his private parts excited by his nurse, who apparently did this to put an irritable child into a good temper! My warning had little effect upon him, as he had become a hopeless victim. He was too delicate a boy for us to desire to keep; and after a brief stay at school, during which we nursed him through a critical illness, he left to finish his education under private tuition at home.

Case D.—This boy came to me at thirteen. He was always a conscientious and amiable boy, but was nervous and dull. By fifteen his dullness had increased, and he complained of brain-strain and poorness of memory. Finally he began to develop St. Vitus's dance. I sent him to our school doctor, who returned him with a note saying that his condition was serious—that he must stop all work, &c. &c. I was in my study when the lad came back, and I at once told him what was the matter. He frankly admitted frequent self-abuse, which he had learned from an elder brother. He had not the least suspicion that the habit was injurious; but was very apprehensive about his future until I reassured him. He wanted me to write at once and warn a younger brother who had fallen into the habit. By great effort he got himself rapidly under control. His nervous twitchings disappeared, his vitality improved, the brain-fag gradually ceased; and when he left, eighteen months later, he was fairly normal. His improvement continued afterwards, and he is now a successful man of business and a married man.

Case E.—This boy entered at twelve. He was very weak physically and highly nervous—owing, his people thought, to severe bullying at a previous school. He was an able boy, of literary and artistic tastes, and almost painfully conscientious. He was very shy; always thought that he was despised by other boys; and was a duffer at games, which he avoided to the utmost. With my present experience I should have known him to be a victim of self-abuse. Then, I did not suspect him; and it was not until he was leaving at eighteen for the University that we talked the matter over, on his initiative. Then I found that he had been bullied into impurity at eleven, and was now a helpless victim. After two years at the University he wrote me that, though the temptation now came less frequently, he seemed absolutely powerless when it did come; that he despised himself so much that the impulse to suicide often haunted him; but that the cowardice which had kept him from games at school would probably prevent his taking his life. With the assistance of an intense and devoted religious life he gradually began to gain self-mastery. It is some years now since he has mentioned the subject to me.

These are merely specimen cases. Cases A, B, and C illustrate my assertions that parents are wonderfully blind; Cases B and E, that quite exceptional refinement in a boy gives no protection from temptation to impurity; Case D, that a boy, even in an extreme case, does not know that the habit is injurious. In respect of their severity, C, D, and E are not normal but extreme cases. The reader must not imagine that boys ordinarily suffer as much as these did.

CHAPTER II.

PREVALENCE OF IMPURITY AMONG BOYS: THE OPINIONS OF CANON LYTTELTON, DR. DUKES, AND OTHERS.

I propose now to make clear to the reader the fact that the conclusions I have reached as to the existence of sexual knowledge among boys, and as to the prevalence of self-abuse, are entirely borne out by the opinion of the most distinguished teachers and medical men.

Canon Lyttelton writes with an authority which no one will question. Educated at Eton, he was for two years an assistant master at Wellington College; then, for fifteen years, headmaster of Haileybury College, and has now been headmaster of Eton for over six years. He has intimate knowledge of boys, derived, as regards the question of purity, from confidential talks with them. The quotations which follow are from his work Training of the Young in Laws of Sex. Canon Lyttelton does not think it needful to make statements as to the prevalence of impurity among boys. He rather assumes that this prevalence is obvious and, under present conditions, inevitable. I have already quoted one passage which involves this assumption, and now invite the reader to consider two others. "In the school life of boys, in spite of very great improvements, it is impossible that sexual subjects should be wholly avoided in common talk.... Though, in preparatory schools of little boys under fourteen, the increasing vigilance of masters, and constant supervision, combined with constant employment, reduce the evil of prurient talk to a minimum, yet these subjects will crop up.... It should be remembered that the boys who are talkative about such subjects are just those whose ideas are most distorted and vicious. In the public school, owing not only to freer talk and more mixed company but to the boy's own wider range of vision, sexual questions, and also those connected with the structure of the body, come to the fore and begin to occupy more or less of the thoughts of all but a peculiarly constituted minority of the whole number.

"Men, as I have shown, have been severely dealt with by Nature in this respect: she has forced them, at a time of life when their minds are ill compacted, their ideas chaotic, and their wills untrained, to face an ordeal which demands above all things reverence based on knowledge and resolution sustained by high affections. An enormously large proportion flounder blindly into the mire before they know what it is, not necessarily, but very often into the defilement of evil habit, but, still more often, into the tainted air of diseased opinion, and after a few years some of them emerge saved, but so as by fire."

The following are quotations from the Upton Letters, written by Mr. A.C. Benson. Mr. Benson is one of the most distinguished of modern teachers: he has had long experience of public-school life both as a boy and as a master: he has that insight into the heart of boyhood which can come only to one who has affectionate sympathy with boys and has been the recipient of their confidences. It will be abundantly evident from the passages which follow that in Mr. Benson's opinion no boy is likely to preserve his "innocence" in passing through a public school.

"The subject is so unpleasant that many masters dare not speak of it at all, and excuse themselves by saying that they don't want to put ideas into boys' heads. I cannot conscientiously believe that a man who has been through a big public school himself can honestly be afraid of that." "The standard of purity is low: a vicious boy does not find his vicious tendencies by any means a bar to social success." This, of course, assumes that the vicious tendencies are a matter of notoriety. A similar implication is involved in the following: "I do not mean to say that there are not many boys who are both pure-minded and honest; but they treat such virtues as a secret preference of their own, and do not consider that it is in the least necessary to interfere with the practice of others or even to disapprove of it." He further gives it as his opinion that "The deadly and insidious temptation of impurity has, as far as one can learn, increased," and tells us "An innocent-minded boy whose natural inclination to purity gave way before perpetual temptation and even compulsion might be thought to have erred, but would have scanty, if any, expression of either sympathy or pity from other boys; while if he breathed the least hint of his miserable position to a master and the fact came out, he would be universally scouted.... One hears of simply heart-rending cases where a boy dare not even tell his parents of what he endures." It would thus appear that in some of the premier schools of the world impurity is a matter of notoriety, sometimes of compulsion; and that, to a boy's own strong inclination to concealment, is superadded, by the public opinion of the school, an imperious command that this concealment shall, even in heart-rending cases, be maintained.

No one, I think, will maintain that private schools as a class are in the least degree lees corrupt than public schools; while there are, I am sure, at least a few schools in which public opinion condemns open impurity, and will not tolerate impure talk. And while I am confident that it is possible, not merely to attain this condition in a school, but also to reduce private impurity to a negligible quantity, impurity — in one form or another — is, in general, so widely spread in boys' schools of every type, that it is difficult to understand how anyone familiar with school life can doubt its prevalence.

Let us now consider the opinion of Dr. Clement Dukes, the medical officer of Rugby School and the greatest English authority on school hygiene. In the preface to the fourth edition of his well-known work Health at School, Dr. Dukes writes: "I have studied children in all their phases and stages for many years — two years at the Hospital for Sick Children in 61 Ormond Street, London, followed by thirty-three years at Rugby School — a professional history which has provided me with an almost unique experience in all that relates to the Health and Disease of Childhood and Youth, and has compelled constant and steady thought upon every aspect of this problem." In an earlier work, The Preservation of Health, Dr. Dukes gives his estimate of the prevalence of masturbation, and quotes the opinion of other authorities whose credentials he has verified; In this work, on page 150, he writes of masturbation: "I believe that the reason why it is so widespread an evil — amounting, I gather, although from the nature of the case no complete evidence can ever be accurately obtained, to somewhere about 90 to 95 per cent. of all boys at boarding-schools — is because the boy leaves his home in the first instance without one word of warning from his parents ... and thus falls into evil ways from his innocence and ignorance alone.... This immorality is estimated by some at 80 per cent., by others at 90 per cent. Another says that not 10 per cent. are innocent. Another that it has always begun at from eight to twelve years of age. Others that it is always worst amongst the elder boys. Others that 'it is universal.'" Professor Stanley Hall, in his great work on Adolescence, after a similar and exhaustive review of the numerous works on this subject in different languages, concludes: "The whole literature on the subject attests that whenever careful researches have been undertaken the results are appalling as to prevalence." And yet there are people who deprecate purity-teaching for boys because they feel that a boy's natural modesty is quite a sufficient protection, and that there is danger of destroying a boy's innocence by putting ideas into his head! To hear such people talk, and to listen to the way in which they speak of self-abuse as though it implied monstrous moral perversion, one would think that the condition of morals when they were young was wholly different. The great novelist Thackeray gives little countenance to this opinion when he writes in Pendennis: "And, by the way, ye tender mothers and sober fathers of Christian families, a prodigious thing that theory of life is as orally learned at a great public school. Why if you could hear those boys of fourteen who blush before mothers and sneak off in silence in the presence of their daughters, talking among each other—it would be the woman's turn to blush then. Before he was twelve years old little Pen had heard talk enough to make him quite awfully wise upon certain points—and so, madam, has your pretty rosy-cheeked son, who is coming home from school for the ensuing holidays. I don't say that the boy is lost, or that the innocence has left him which he had from 'Heaven, which is our home,' but that the shades of the prison-house are closing fast over him, and that we are helping as much as possible to corrupt him."

Before concluding this chapter I would caution the reader against the error of supposing that the opinions expressed by Canon Lyttelton and Dr. Dukes are indicative merely of the conditions they have met at Haileybury, Eton, and Rugby. They are equally significant of the conditions which obtain in the innumerable schools from which Haileybury, Eton, and Rugby are recruited; and as there is no reason why other preparatory schools should differ from these, they are significant of the almost universal condition of boys' schools.

CHAPTER III.
CAUSES OF THE PREVALENCE OF IMPURITY AMONG BOYS.

The evidence I have adduced in the previous chapters will convince most of my readers that few boys retain their innocence after they are of school age. There may, however, be a few who find it impossible to reconcile this conclusion with their ideas of boy nature. I will therefore now examine current conceptions on this subject and expose their fundamental inaccuracy.

There are some people who imagine that a boy's innate modesty is quite sufficient protection against defilement. Does experience really warrant any such conclusion? Those who know much of children will recognise the fact that even the cardinal virtues of truthfulness and honesty have often to be learned, and that ideas of personal cleanliness, of self-restraint in relation to food, and of consideration for others have usually to be implanted and fostered. Among people of refinement these virtues are often so early learned that there is danger lest we should consider them innate. The susceptibility of some children to suggestions conveyed to them by the example and precept of their elders is almost unlimited. Hence a child may, at two, have given up the trick of clearing its nostrils with the finger-nail, and may, before five, have learned most of the manners and virtues of refined people. The majority, however, take longer to learn these things, so that a jolly little chap of ten or twelve is often by no means scrupulously clean in hands, nails, ears, and teeth, is often distinctly greedy, and sometimes far from truthful.

That cleanliness and virtue are acquired and not innate is obvious enough from the fact that children who grow up among dirty and unprincipled people are rarely clean and virtuous. Were it possible for the child of refined parents to grow up without example or precept in relation to table manners and morals, except the example and advice of vulgar people, who would expect refinement and consideration from him? Is there anyone who has such faith in innate refinement that he would be content to let a child of his own, grow up without a hint on these matters, and with such example only as was supplied by association with vulgar people? Yet this is precisely what we do in relation to the subject of personal purity. The child has no good example to guide him. The extent to which temptation comes to those whom he respects, the manner in which they comport themselves when tempted, the character of their sex relations are entirely hidden from him. He is not only without example, he is without precept. No ideals are set before him, no advice is given to him: the very existence of anything in which ideals and advice are needful is ignored.

If in conditions like these we should expect a boy to grow up greedy, we may be certain that he will grow up impure. At puberty there awakes within him by far the strongest appetite that human nature can experience—an appetite against which some of the noblest of mankind have striven in vain. The appetite is given abnormal strength by the artificial and stimulating conditions under which he lives. The act which satisfies this appetite is also one of keen pleasure. He has long been accustomed to caress his private parts, and the pleasure with which he does this is greatly enhanced. He does not suspect that indulgence is harmful. This pleasure, unlike that of eating, costs him nothing, and is ever available. His powers of self-control are as yet undeveloped. He can indulge himself without incurring the least suspicion. He probably knows that most boys, of his age and above, indulge themselves. The result is inevitable. He finds that sexual thoughts are keenly pleasurable, and that they produce bodily exaltation. He has much yet to learn on the subject of sex, and he enjoys the quest. Wherever he turns he finds it now—in his Bible, in animal life, in his classics, in the encyclopædia, in his companions, and in the newspaper. Day and night the subject is ever with him. It is inevitable. And at this juncture comes along the theorist who is aghast at our destroying the lad's "innocence," and at our "suggesting evils to him which otherwise he would never have thought of." "The boy's innate modesty is quite a sufficient protection"!

To me the wonderful thing is the earnestness with which a boy sets about the task of cleansing his life when once he has been made to realise the real character of the thoughts and acts with which he has been playing. Boys, as I find them, rarely err in this matter, or in any other, from moral perversity, but merely from ignorance and thoughtlessness. Severe rebukes and punishments are rarely either just or useful. The disposition which obliges the teacher to use them in the last resort, and the rebellion against authority which is said to follow puberty, arise almost invariably from injudicious training in the home or at school. Boys who have received a fair home training, and who find themselves in a healthy atmosphere at school, are almost invariably delightful to deal with; and even those who have been less fortunate in their early surroundings adapt themselves in most cases to the standards which a healthy public opinion in the school demands.

It may be thought that the mere reticence of adults about reproduction and the reproductive organs would impress the child's mind with the idea that it is unclean to play with his private parts or to talk about their functions with his companions. This is a psychological error. For some years past adults have avoided any allusion to the subject of excretion, and the child assumes that public attention to bodily needs and public reference to these needs are alike indelicate. He does not, however, conclude that excretion in private is an indelicate act, nor does any sense of delicacy oblige him to maintain, with regard to companions of his own sex and age, the reticence which has become habitual to him in his relations with adults. Why should the child think it "dirty" to fondle and excite his private parts or to talk about them with his boy friends? The knowledge which makes us feel as we do is as yet hidden from him.

The same thing is certainly true of conversation about the facts of reproduction when those who converse are uncorrupted. Another element, however, at once appears when these facts are divulged by a corrupt boy, because his manner is irresistibly suggestive of uncleanness as well as of secrecy. Similarly when self-abuse is fallen into spontaneously by a boy who is otherwise clean, no sense of indecency attaches itself to the act. When, however, it is taught by an unclean boy, there is a feeling of defilement from the first. In boys under the age of puberty this feeling may overpower the temptation; in boys above that age it is, as a rule, totally inadequate as a safeguard.

Many people imagine that a boy who is impure must betray himself, and that if no overt acts of indecency are observed the innocence of a boy's mind may be safely inferred. Knowledge on these subjects has, however, been almost invariably gained under conditions of the utmost secrecy, and the behaviour of adults has effectively fostered the idea of concealment. Hence we might expect that the secret would be jealously guarded and that any overt act of impurity would be avoided in the presence of adults with even greater circumspection than the public performance of an excretory act. The habit of self-abuse, moreover, is practised usually under the double cover of darkness and the bed-clothes. The temptation occurs far less by day than by night, and a boy who yields to it in the day invariably chooses a closet or other private place in which he feels secure from detection.

To many people it is inconceivable that a lad can harbour impure feelings and habits without obvious deterioration; but even if a child's lapses into these things were associated with conscious guilt, does our knowledge of human nature justify us in supposing that evil in the heart is certain to betray itself in a visible degradation of the outer life? If we believe the language of the devout, we must admit that the most spiritual of men hide in their heart thoughts of which they are heartily ashamed. It is not into the mouth of the reprobate but into the mouth of her devoted members as they enter upon their sacramental service that the Church puts the significant prayer, "Almighty God, unto whom all hearts be open, all desires known, and from whom no secrets are hid; Cleanse the thoughts in our hearts by the inspiration of thy Holy Spirit." Inconsistency in adults is far too well recognised to need proof. In children it is even more obvious, and for this reason that, looked at aright, it is the faculty of maintaining the general health of the soul, spite of local morbid conditions—a faculty which is strongest in the simpler and more adaptable mind of the child.

Impurity as a disease has a long incubation period. When he contracts the disease, its victim is often wholly unconscious of his danger; and, both because the disease is an internal one and is slow in development, it is a very long time before obvious symptoms appear. Meanwhile a corruption may have set in which will ultimately ruin the whole life.

CHAPTER IV.
RESULTS OF YOUTHFUL IMPURITY.

It is difficult to exaggerate the evils which result from the present system under which boys grow to manhood without any adult guidance in relation to the laws of sex.

It has already been stated that the immediate physical results of self-abuse are small evils indeed compared with the corruption of mind which comes from perverted sex ideas. They are, however, by no means negligible; and are, in some cases, very serious. The great prevalence of self-abuse among boys, combined with the inevitable uncertainty as to the degree of a boy's freedom from, or indulgence in, this vice, makes it very difficult to institute a reliable comparison between those who are chaste and those who are unchaste. Greater significance attaches, I think, to a comparison in individual cases of a boy's condition during a period of indulgence in masturbation and his condition after its total, or almost total, relinquishment. I have no hesitation in saying that the difference in a boy's vitality and spiritual tone after relinquishing this habit is very marked. The case D quoted in Chapter I. is, in this respect, typical.

In my pamphlet, Private Knowledge for Boys, I have quoted a striking passage from Acton on the Reproductive Organs, in which he contrasts the continent and the incontinent boy. But in the case of men like Dr. Acton—specialists in the diseases of the male reproductive organs—it must be remembered that it is mostly the abnormal and extreme cases which come under their notice: a fact which is liable to affect their whole estimate. The book can be recommended to adults who wish to see the whole subject of sex diseases dealt with by a specialist who writes with a high moral purpose.

My own estimate is given in the pamphlet already referred to. After quoting Dr. Acton's opinion, I add:—

"You will notice that Dr. Acton is here describing an extreme case. I want to tell you what are the results in a case which is not extreme. My difficulty is that these results are so various. The injury to the nerves and brain which is caused by sexual excitement and by the loss of semen leaves nothing in the body, mind or character uninjured. The extent of the injury varies greatly with the strength of a boy's constitution and with the frequency of his sin. The character of the injury varies with the boy's own special weaknesses and tendencies. If he is naturally shy and timid, it makes him shyer and more timid. If he is stupid and lazy, it makes him more stupid and lazy. If he is inclined to consumption or other disease, it destroys his power of resisting such disease. In extreme cases only does it actually change an able boy into a stupid one, an athletic boy into a weak one, and a happy boy into a discontented one; but in all cases it weakens every power a boy possesses. Its most prominent results are these: loss of will-power and self-reliance, shyness, nervousness and irritability, failure of the reasoning powers and memory, laziness of body and mind, a diseased fondness for girls, deceitfulness. Of these results, the loss of will-power leaves the boy a prey not only to the temptations of impurity, but to every other form of temptation: the deceitfulness destroys his self-respect and turns his life into a sham."

Of incomparably greater importance than Acton's wide but abnormal experience and my own narrow but normal experience is the experience of Dr. Clement Dukes, which is very wide and perfectly normal. No man has probably been in so good a position for forming an estimate as he has been. Dr. Dukes thus sums up his opinion: "The harm which results is moral, intellectual, and physical. Physicallyit is a frequent drain at a critical time of life when nature is providing for growth and development, and is ill able to bear it; it is a powerful nervous shock to the system ill-prepared to meet it.... It also causes muscular and mental debility, loss of spirit and manliness, and occasional insanity, suicide and homicide. Moreover it leads to further uncontrollable passions in early manhood.... Further, this vice enfeebles the intellectual powers, inducing lethargy and obtuseness, and incapacity for hard mental work. And last, and most of all, it is an immorality which stains the whole character and undermines the life."

In this passage Dr. Dukes refers to the intellectual and moral harm of self-abuse as well as to its physical consequences. Intimately connected as these are with one another, I am here attempting to give them separate treatment. It is, however, impossible to treat perverted sex-knowledge and self-abuse separately; for though in young boys they are found independently of one another, and sometimes co-exist in elder boys without any intimate conscious association, their results are identical. In the following pages, therefore, I shall refer to them jointly as impurity.

The earliest evil which springs from impurity is the destruction of the intimacy which has hitherto existed between the boy and his parents. Closely associated with this is that duplicity of life which results from secrets which may be shared with the coarse but must be jealously concealed from everyone who is respected. Untold harm follows these changes in a lad. Hitherto he has had nothing to conceal from his mother — unless, indeed, his parents have been foolish enough to drive him into deception by undue severity over childish mistakes, and accidents, and moral lapses. Every matter which has occupied his thoughts he has freely shared with those who can best lead him into the path of moral health.

Henceforth all is changed. The lad has his own inner life which he must completely screen from the kind eyes which have hitherto been his spiritual lights. Concealment is soon found to be an easy thing. Acts and words are things of which others may take cognisance; the inner life no one can ever know. A world is opened to the lad in which the restraints of adult opinion are not felt at all and the guidance and inspiration of a father's or mother's love never come. How completely this is the case in regard to impurity the reader will hardly doubt if he remembers that all parents believe their boys to be innocent, and that some 90 per cent. of them are hopelessly hoodwinked. But this double life is not long confined to the subject of purity. The concealment which serves one purpose excellently can be made to serve another; and henceforth parents and adult friends need never know anything but what they are told. It is a sad day for the mother when first she realises that the old frankness has gone; it is a very, very much sadder day for the boy. There is no fibre of his moral being but is, or will be, injured by this divorce of home influences and by this ever-accumulating burden of guilty memories. "His mother may not know why this is so," writes Canon Lyttelton; "the only thing she may be perfectly certain of is that the loss will never be quite made up as long as life shall last."

Another injury done by impurity to the growing mind of the lad is that, in all matters relating to sex, he learns to look merely for personal enjoyment. In every other department of life he is moved by a variety of motives: by the desire to please, the desire to excel, by devotion to duty, by the love of truth, and by many other desires. Even in gratifying the appetite most nearly on the same plane as the sexual appetite—namely, that of hunger—he has more or less regard for his own well-being, more or less consideration for the wishes of others, and a constant desire to attain the standard expected of him. Meanwhile, as regards the sexual appetite—the racial importance of which is great; and the regulation of which is of infinite importance for himself, for those who may otherwise become its victims, for the wife he may one day wed, and for the children, legitimate or illegitimate, that he may beget—his one idea is personal enjoyment. One deplorable result of this idea will be adverted to in the next chapter.

When boyish impurity involves a coarse way of looking at sexual relations, as it always must when these are matters of common talk and jest, the boy suffers a loss which prejudicially affects the whole tone of his mind and every department of his conduct—I mean the loss of reverence. It is those things alone which are sacred to us, those things about which we can talk only with friends, and about which we can jest with no one, that have inspiration in them, that can give us power to follow our ideals and to lay a restraining hand on the brute within us. Fortunately the self-control which manifests itself in heroism, in good form, and in the sportsmanlike spirit is sacred to almost all. To most, a mother's love is sacred. To many, all that is implied in the word religion. To a few, sexual passion and the great manifestations of human genius in poetry, music, painting, sculpture, and architecture. Exactly in proportion as these things are profaned by jest and mockery, is the light of the soul quenched and man degraded to the level of the beast. Considering how large a part the sex-passion plays in the lives of most men and women; considering how it permeates the literature and art of the World and is—as the basis of the home—the most potent factor in social life, its profanation is a terrible loss, and the habit of mind which such profanation engenders cannot fail to weaken the whole spirit of reverence. I must confess that the man who jests over sex relations is to me incomparably lower than the man who sustains clean but wholly illegitimate sex relations; and while I am conscious of a strong movement of friendship towards a lad who has admitted impurity in his life but retains reverence for purity, it is hard to feel anything but repulsion towards one who profanes the subject of sex with coarse and ribald talk.

As a result of the two evils of which I have now spoken, together with the physical effects of masturbation, young men become powerless to face the sexual temptations of manhood; and many, who in all other relations of life are admirable, sink in this matter into the mire of prostitution or the less demoralising, but far crueller, sin of seduction.

Thrown on the streets, usually through no fault of her own, often merely from an over-trustful love, the prostitute sinks to the lowest depths of degradation and despair. It is not merely that she sells to every comer, clean or bestial, without even the excuse of appetite or of passion, what should be yielded alone to love; but it is also that to do this she poisons body and mind with spirit-drinking, leads a life of demoralising indolence and self-indulgence, is cut off from all decent associations, and sinks, under the combined influence of these things and of fell disease, into a loathsome creature whom not the lowest wants; sinks into destitution, misery, suicide, or the outcast's early grave. Writing of the young man who is familiar with London, the Headmaster of Eton says: "He cannot fail to see around him a whole world of ruined life—a ghastly varnish of gaiety spread over immeasurable tracts of death and corruption; a state of things so heart-rending and so hopeless that on calm consideration of it the brain reels, and sober-minded people who, from motives of pity, have looked the hideous evil in the face, have asserted that nothing in their experience has seemed to threaten them so nearly with a loss of reason."

Into the contamination of this inferno, into active support of this cruel infamy, many and many a young man is led by the impurity of his boyhood. Such at least is the conclusion of some who know boys best. Thus Dr. Dukes writes:

"This evil, of which I have spoken so long and so freely, is, I believe, the root of the evil of prostitution and similar vices; and if this latter evil is to be mitigated, it can only be, to my mind, by making the life of the schoolboy purer.

"How is it possible to put a stop to this terrible social evil? How is it possible to elevate women while the demand for them for base purposes is so great? We must go to the other end of the scale and make men better; we must train young boys more in purity of life and chastity BEFORE their passions become uncontrollable.

"Whereas the cry of every moralist and philanthropist is, 'Let us put a stop to this prostitution, open and clandestine.' This cannot be effected at present, much as it is to be desired; the demand for it is too great, even possibly greater than the supply. If we wish to eradicate it, we must go to the fountainhead and make those who create the demand purer, so that, the demand falling off, the supply will be curtailed."

To this I venture to add that by teaching chastity we not merely decrease the demand for prostitutes, but we greatly diminish the supply. Few girls, if any, take to the streets until they have been seduced; and the antecedents of seduction are the morbid exaggeration of the sexual appetite, the lack of self-control, and the selfish hedonism which youthful impurity engenders.

The selfishness, and consequent blindness to cruelty, of which I write, manifests itself quite early. A boy of chivalrous feeling, whose blood would boil at any other form of outrage on a girl, will read a newspaper account of rape or indecent assault with a pleasure so intense that indignation and disgust are quite crowded out of his mind.

If, repelled by the coarseness of the streets, the young man allows lust or passion to lead him into seduction, he commits a crime the consequences of which are usually cruel in the extreme; for in most cases the seduced girl sinks of necessity into prostitution. So blind, so callous does impurity make even the refined and generous, that many a young man who can be a good son, a good brother, a noble friend, a patriotic citizen, will doom a girl whose only fault is that she is physically attractive—and possibly too affectionate and trusting—to torturing anxiety, to illness, to the horrible suffering of undesired travail, to disgrace, and in nineteen cases out of twenty to ostracism and the infamy of the streets. Murder is a small thing compared with this. Who would not rather that his daughter were killed in her innocence than that she should be doomed to such a fate?

Many young men are ignorant of the fact that sexual relations with prostitutes frequently result in the foulest and most terrible of diseases. Venereal diseases, as these are called, commence in the private parts themselves, but the poison which they engender soon attacks other parts of the body and often wrecks the general health. It gives rise to loathsome skin disease, to degeneration of the nervous system and paralysis, to local disease in the heart, lungs, and digestive organs, and to such lowering of vitality as renders the body an easy prey to disease generally. No one is justified in looking upon this risk as a matter of merely private concern. Health is of supreme importance not merely to the personal happiness and success of the man himself, but also to the services he can render to his friends, to his nation, and to humanity. Even if a young man is foolish enough to risk his happiness and success for the sake of animal enjoyment, he cannot without base selfishness and disloyalty disregard the duties he owes to others. Further, the man who suffers from venereal disease is certain to pass its poison on to his wife and children—cursing thus with unspeakable misery those whom of all others it is his duty to protect and bless.

One cannot help feeling at times that the blessings of home—and of the monogamy which makes home possible—are terribly discounted by a condition of things which offer a young man no other alternatives to chastity than these terrible evils. Now that year by year the rising standard of living and the increased exactions which the State makes on the industrious and provident cause marriage to be a luxury too expensive for many, and delayed unduly for most, the problem of social purity becomes ever greater and more urgent. The instruction of the young in relation to sex provides the only solution, and is, I venture to think, incomparably the most important social reform now needed.

I am confident that a boy who receives wise training and sex guidance from his early days will never find lust the foul and uncontrollable element which it is to-day in the lives of most men; that in a few generations our nation could be freed from the seething corruption which poisons its life; and that, while freer scope could be given to the ineffable joys of pure sexual love, very much could be done to diminish the awful misery and degradation engendered by lust.

If children had from their infancy an instinctive and growing desire for alcohol, with secret and unrestrained means of gratifying it; if by its indulgence this desire grew into an overmastering craving; if throughout childhood they received no word of warning or guidance from the good, but were tempted and corrupted by the evil, we should have a nation in which most men and women were drunkards, ready to break all laws — human and divine — which stood in the way of an imperious need; a nation in which, among those who declined to yield to iniquity, the craving for drink caused unceasing and life-long struggle.

On the young man of to-day we lay a burden which no ordinary man was ever yet able to bear. His boyhood and youth become, through ignorance, the prey of lust; his passions become tyrannous; his will is enslaved. Even if he contracts marriage, his troubles are not at an end, for man, as an animal, is neither monogamous nor wholly constant. His neglected sex-education makes him far more susceptible to physical attractions than to those qualities which make a wife a good companion, a good housekeeper, and a good mother; and but too often, as a result, the beneficent influence of marriage is transient; the domestic atmosphere ceases to be congenial; both husband and wife become susceptible to other attachments, and the old struggle begins all over again.

CHAPTER V.

SEX KNOWLEDGE IS COMPATIBLE WITH PERFECT REFINEMENT AND INNOCENCE.

The reader who has followed me through the preceding chapters will, I hope, feel that, whatever objections there may be to giving explicit instruction on sex matters to the young, such instruction is immensely to be preferred to the almost inevitable perversion which follows ignorance. If we had to choose between a state of "innocence" and a state of reverent knowledge, many people would doubtless incline to the former. No such option exists. Our choice lies between leaving a lad to pick up information from vulgar and unclean minds, and giving it ourselves in such a manner as to invest it from the first with sacredness and dignity.

Even if the reader is still inclined to think that sex-knowledge is, at best, an unholy secret, he will hardly doubt that it can be divulged with less injury by an adult who is earnestly anxious for the child's welfare than by coarse and irreverent lips.

I am not content to leave the reader in this dilemma. I am confident that the following words of Canon Lyttelton spring from the truest spiritual insight: "To a lover of nature, no less than to a convinced Christian, the subject ought to wear an aspect not only negatively innocent, but positively beautiful. It is a recurrent miracle, and yet the very type and embodiment of law; and it may be confidently affirmed that, in spite of the blundering of many generations, there is nothing in a normally-constituted child's mind which refuses to take in the subject from this point of view, provided that the right presentation of it is the first."

Nothing more forcibly convicts the present system of the evil which lies at its door than the current beliefs on this subject. At present, sexual knowledge is picked up from the gutter and the cesspool; and no purification can free it entirely in many minds from its original uncleanness.

"Love's a virtue for heroes! — as white as the snow on high hills,

And immortal as every great soul is that struggles, endures, and fulfils."

This is the prophet's belief, and yet, putting on one side those who actually delight in uncleanness, there appear to be many people who look upon the marriage certificate as a licence to impurity, and upon sexual union as a form of animal indulgence to which we are so strongly impelled that even the most refined are tempted by it into an act of conscious indelicacy and sin. Such people read literally the psalmist's words: "Behold, I was shapen in iniquity, and in sin did my mother conceive me." It is surely some such feeling as this which makes parents shrink from referring to the subject, which underlies the constant use of the word "innocence" as the aptest description of a state of mind which precedes the acquisition of sexual knowledge.

That individuals, at least, have risen to a loftier conception than this is certain; and the only possible explanations of the prevalence of the current idea are that sex-knowledge has almost always been obtained from a tainted source; and that, while the coarse have not merely whispered their views in the ear in the closet, but have, in all ages, proclaimed them from the house-tops, the refined have hardly whispered their ideas, much less discussed them publicly. Children growing up with perverted views have listened to the loud assertions of disputants on the one side, have witnessed the demoralisation which so often attends the sexual passion, but have received no hint of what may be said on the other side of the question.

An instructed public opinion would be horrified at our sovereign's taking shares in a slave-trading expedition as Queen Elizabeth did. We are aghast at the days when crowds went forth to enjoy the torture at the stake of those from whom they differed merely on some metaphysical point. We have even begun to be restless under man's cruel domination over the animal creation. But we have made far less advance in our conceptions on sexual matters; and we are content here with ideas which were current in Elizabethan days. But for this, no passion for conservatism, no reverence for a liturgy endeared by centuries of use, could induce us to tell every bride as she stands before God's altar that it is one of her functions to provide an outlet for her husband's passion and a safeguard against fornication. Lust is at least as degrading in married life as it is outside it. No legal contract, no religious ceremony, can purify, much less sanctify, what is essentially impure.

Those who desire to assist in the uplifting of humanity cannot afford to be silent and to allow judgment to go against them by default. Courage they will need; for a charge of indecency is sure to be levelled against them by the indecent, and they may be misjudged even by the pure.

This is not the place in which so delicate a matter can be fully discussed, nor does space permit; but if the movement towards sex instruction is not to be stultified by the very ideas which evidence the need for it, the subject cannot be wholly ignored here, and I venture to throw out a few suggestions.

Are we indeed to believe that the noblest and most spiritual of men will compromise themselves in the eyes of the woman they love best, and whose respect they most desire, by committing in her presence and making her the instrument of an indelicate act? A great poet, who remained an ardent lover and a devoted companion until his wife died in his arms—blissfully happy that she might die so—has written:

"Let us not always say,

'Spite of the flesh to-day

I strove, made head, gained ground upon the whole.'

As the bird wings and sings,

Let us cry, 'All good things

Are ours, nor soul helps flesh more, now, than flesh helps soul.'"

Again: are we, who believe in a Divine government of the world, able to imagine that God has made the perpetuation of the race dependent upon acts of sin or of indelicacy? Did He who graced with His presence the marriage at Cana in Galilee really countenance a ceremony which was a prelude to sin? Did He who took the little children in His arms and blessed them know, as He said "for of such is the kingdom of heaven," that not one of them could have existed without indelicacy, and that they were but living proof of their fathers' lapses and their mothers' humiliation? Is He whom we address daily as "Our Father" willing to be described by a name with which impurity is of necessity connected? And has He implanted in us as the strongest of our instincts that which cannot elevate and must debase?

Again: it needs no wide experience of life, nor any very indulgent view of it, to feel some truth at least in the words Tennyson puts into the mouth of his ideal man:

"Indeed I knew

Of no more subtle master under heaven

Than is the maiden passion for a maid

Not only to keep down the base in man,

But teach high thought, and amiable words,

And courtliness, and the desire for fame,

And love of truth, and all that makes a man."

And yet this passion is indisputably sexual passion, and the chastest of lovers has bodily proof that the most spiritual of his kisses is allied to the supreme embrace of love. Our body is the instrument by which all our emotions are expressed. The most obvious way of expressing affection is by bodily contact. The mother fondles her child, kisses its lips and its limbs, and presses it to her breast. Young children hold hands, put their arms round one another and kiss; and, although later we become less demonstrative, we still take our friend's arm, press his hand with ours, and lay a hand upon his shoulder; we pat our horse or dog and stroke our cat. The lover returns to the spontaneous and unrestrained caresses of his childhood. These become more and more intimate until they find their consummation in the most intimate and most sacred of all embraces. From first to last these caresses—however deep the pleasure they bestow—are sought by the mother or the lover, not for the sake of that pleasure, but as a means of expressing emotion. He only who realises this fact and conforms to it can enter on married life with any certainty of happiness. The happiness of very many marriages is irretrievably shattered at the outset through the craving for sexual excitement which, in the absence of wise guidance, grows up in every normal boy's heart, and by the contemplation of sexual intercourse as an act of physical pleasure.

And once again: It is the experience of those who have given instruction in sex questions to the young that by those whose minds have never been defiled the instruction is received with instant reverence, as something sacred; not with shame, as something foul. I venture once more to quote Canon Lyttelton, who sets forth his experience and my own in language the beauty of which I cannot imitate:

"There is something awe-inspiring in the innocent readiness of little children to learn the explanation of by far the greatest fact within the horizon of their minds. The way they receive it, with native reverence, truthfulness of understanding, and guileless delicacy, is nothing short of a revelation of the never-ceasing bounty of Nature, who endows successive generations of children with this instinctive ear for the deep harmonies of her laws. People sometimes speak of the indescribable beauty of children's innocence, and insist that there is nothing which calls for more constant thanksgiving than that influence on mankind. But I will venture to say that no one quite knows what it is who has foregone the privilege of being the first to set before them the true meaning of life and birth and the mystery of their own being."

To the arguments thus briefly indicated it is no answer to say that sexual union is essentially physical, and that to regard it in any other way is transcendental. Among primitive men eating and drinking were merely animal. We have made them, in our meals, an accompaniment to social pleasures, and in our religious life we have raised them to a sacramental level.

CHAPTER VI.

CONDITIONS UNDER WHICH PURITY TEACHING IS BEST GIVEN: REMEDIAL AND CURATIVE MEASURES.

We have now seen that impurity is almost universal among boys who have been left without warning and instruction; that, under these conditions, it is practically inevitable; that its direct results are lowered vitality and serious injury to character, its indirect results an appalling amount of degradation and misery; finally, that there is nothing in sex knowledge, when rightly presented, which can in the least defile a child's mind. All that now remains is for us to consider by whom and under what circumstances instruction on this subject should be given, and what assistance can be rendered to boys who desire to lead chaste lives.

Without doubt, instruction should be given to a boy by his parents in the home. When young children ask questions with regard to reproduction, parents should neither ignore these question nor give the usual silly answers. If the occasion on which the question is asked is not one in which an answer can appropriately be given, the child should be gently warned that the question raised is one about which people do not openly talk, and the promise of an answer hereafter should be made. Then, at the first convenient hour, the child can either be given the information he seeks or told that he shall hear all about the matter at some future specified time, as for example, his sixth or eighth birthday.

In the absence of questions from a child, the ideal thing would be for the child, at the age of six, seven, or eight, to learn orally from his mother the facts of maternity and to receive warning against playing with his private parts. Whether at this time it is best to teach him the facts of paternity is, I think, doubtful. Canon Lyttelton is strongly of opinion that the father's share in the child's existence should be explained when the mother's share is explained, and there is much weight in what he says. If the question of paternity is reserved, it should not be on the ground that there is anything embarrassing or indelicate about the matter, and, when the facts are revealed, the child should clearly understand that they have been withheld merely until his mind was sufficiently developed to understand them. The only safe guide in such matters is experience, and of this as yet we have unfortunately little.

The question next arises: should it be the mother or the father who gives this instruction? As regards the earlier part of the instruction a confident reply can be made to this question. The information should be given by the parent whose relations with the child are the more intimate and tender, and whose influence over him is the greater. This will, of course, usually be the mother. The subject of paternity may, if reserved for future treatment, be appropriately given by the father, provided that he and his son are on really intimate terms. If timely warning is given to a child about playing with his private parts, no reference need be made to self-abuse until a boy leaves home for school, or until he is nearing the age of puberty.

There are many mothers whose insight and tact will enable them to approach these questions in the best possible way and to say exactly the right thing. There are others—a large majority, I think—who would be glad of guidance, and there are not a few who would certainly leave the matter alone unless thus guided. It was mainly to assist parents in this work that I published last year a pamphlet entitled Private Knowledge for Boys. This embodies just what, in my opinion, should be said to an intelligent child, and it has, in my own hands, proved effective for many years past. In the case of young children the teaching should certainly be oral, provided that the mother knows clearly what to say, has sufficient powers of expression to say it well, and can talk without any feeling of embarrassment. Unless these conditions co-exist I recommend the use of a pamphlet. As I have found that children often do not know what one means by the "private parts," I make this clear at the outset.

Some into whose hands this book may come and who have boys of twelve and upwards to whom they have never given instruction, may possibly be glad of advice as to the manner in which the subject can best be dealt with in their case. For boys of this age, I am strongly of opinion that it is better in most cases to make use of a pamphlet than to attempt oral instruction. Probably they already have some knowledge on the subject; possibly some sense of guilt. If so, it will be found very difficult to treat the matter orally without embarrassment—a thing to be avoided at all costs. I was interested to find that on receipt of my pamphlet Professor Geddes—one of the greatest experts on sex—placed it at once in the hands of his own boy, a fact from which his opinion on the relative merits of oral and printed instruction can easily be inferred.

Many of my readers who have boys of fourteen and upwards to whom they have hitherto given no instruction will, I hope, feel that they must now do this. I venture, therefore, to give a detailed account of the manner in which I should myself act in similar circumstances. I should arrange to be with the lad when there was no danger of interruption, and in such circumstances as would put him at his ease. I should tell him that I was conscious of unwisdom in not speaking to him before about a subject of supreme importance to him; that I took upon myself all blame for anything he might, in ignorance, have said or done; that through ignorance I had myself fallen and suffered, and that I should like him now to sit down and read through this pamphlet slowly and carefully. When he finished I should try by every possible means to make him sensible of my affection for him. I should associate myself in a few words with the sentiments of the writer, and should invite the lad to tell me whether he had fallen into temptation, and if so to what extent. A confidence of this kind assists a boy greatly and establishes a delightful intimacy.

There are several points with regard to purity-teaching which need to be emphasised.

Such teaching can hardly be too explicit. "Beating about the bush" is always indicative of the absence of self-possession. The embarrassment manifested is quickly perceived even by a young child, and is certain to communicate itself to the recipient. It is of paramount importance that the child should, from the first, feel that the knowledge imparted is pure; anything which suggests that it is indelicate should be studiously avoided. The introduction of a few science terms is advantageous in several ways: amongst others it relieves the tension which the spiritual aspect of the question may engender, it gives a lad a terminology which is free from filthy contamination.

It is important that the information given should be full, otherwise the boy lives in a chronic state of curiosity, which, to his great detriment, he is ever trying to satisfy. If the reader feels that the information is dangerous, and aims, therefore, at imparting as little as possible, he is not fitted to do the work at all.

No greater mistake can be made than that of taxing a boy with impurity as though it were a conscious and egregious fault. I have already expressed my strong opinion that, in almost every instance, the boy is a victim to be sympathised with, not a culprit to be punished. This opinion is shared, I believe, by everyone who has investigated the subject. It is certainly the opinion of Canon Lyttelton and Dr. Dukes. It is, indeed, easy to exaggerate the conscious guilt even of boys who have initiated others into masturbation. Apart from the injustice to the boy of an attitude of severity, it is certain to shut the boy's heart up with a snap.

If a pamphlet is used it should, without fail, be taken from a boy when he has read it. Much harm may, I fear, result from supplying boys with the cheap pamphlets which well-meaning but inexperienced persons are producing.

Should the time ever come when parents give timely warning and instruction to boys, a very difficult problem will be solved for the schoolmaster. But in the meantime what ought the schoolmaster to do? The following plan commends itself to some eminent teachers. As soon as a boy is about to enter the school a letter is sent to his parents advising them to give the boy instruction, and a pamphlet is enclosed for this purpose. This plan has the decided advantage of shifting the responsibility on to the shoulders of those who ought to take it. The weakness of the plan arises from the fact that most parents do not believe in the prevalence of impurity among boys, and are quite confident that their own boys need no warning. Hence they may do nothing at all, or merely content themselves with some vague and quite useless statement.

The traditions of most boys' schools make it impossible for those intimate and respectful relations to exist between masters and boys without which confidential teaching of this kind may be even worse than useless. Where masters are invariably referred to disrespectfully if not contemptuously, where a teacher's most earnest address is a "jaw" which the recipient is expected to betray and mock at with his companions; where to shield profanity, indecency, and bullying from detection is the imperative duty of every boy below the Sixth; where failure to avert from a moral leper the kindly treatment which might restore him to health and prevent the wholesale infection of others is the one unpardonable sin, only one or two teachers of a generation can hope to do much, and the risk of failure is immense. I can hardly believe that the present race of teachers will long tolerate the system I here advert to. Public opinion canbe organised and enlisted as strongly on the side of Right as it is now, but too often, on the side of Evil. Mr. A.C. Benson is very moderate when he writes: "To take no steps to arrive at such an organisation, and to leave it severely alone, is a very dark responsibility."

Even in such a school, some good is, I know, done by tactful public references to the existence of masturbation and to its deplorable consequences.

The question is not free from difficulty even when the general atmosphere of the school is healthy and helpful. If one dared to leave this instruction until the age of puberty, the lad would be capable of a much deeper impression than he is at an earlier age, and the impression would be fresh just at the time at which it is most needed. In the case of boys who have come to me at nine or ten I have sometimes ventured to defer my interview for four or five years, and have found them quite uncorrupted. On the other hand, within an hour of penning these lines I have been talking to a little boy of eleven who commenced masturbation two years ago while he was under excellent home influence. One such boy may, without guilt, corrupt a whole set, for impurity is one of the most infectious as well as the most terrible of diseases. The ideal state in a school is not reached until periodical addresses on purity can be given to all with the certainty that by all they will be listened to and treated reverently and respectfully. Such addresses cannot well be made the vehicle of sex information, but they can be so constructed as to guide those to whom individual instruction has not yet been given, and to strengthen those who, spite of full instruction, periodically need a helping hand.

What results may we reasonably expect from adequate and timely instruction? I have so rarely met a case in which this has been given at home that I can only infer what these results might be from the cases in which my own instruction has been given in time. In almost every instance I feel sure that the results have been beneficial, that the temptation to impurity has been little felt, and that a healthy and chaste boyhood has resulted. Canon Lyttelton writes: "The influences of school life have been found to be impotent to deprave the tone of a boy who has been fortified by the right kind of instruction from his parents." This I can well believe, for, if the schoolmaster can do much, there can be no limit to a power which has been cradled in the sanctity of home and cherished by a mother's love. This appears to be the emphatic opinion also of Dr. Dukes. Of a boy thus favoured, Canon Lyttelton writes: "He will feel that any rude handling of such a theme, even of only its outer fringe, is like the profaning of the Holy of Holies in his heart, and he will no more suffer it than he would suffer a stranger to defile the innermost shrine of his feelings by taking his mother's or his sister's name in vain. All the goading curiosity which drives other boys to pry greedily into nature's laws, in blank ignorance of their mighty import, their unspeakable depth, and spiritual unearthly harmonies, has been for him forestalled, enlightened, and purified."

It is a sad step down from such a boy to the lad who has been given warning after corruption has begun. Most boys feel such shame in confessing to failure that one has to accept with reserve the statements made by even the most truthful of those who are treading the upward path. After making due allowance for this source of error, my experience enables me to say confidently that, if a boy has notbeen long or badly corrupted, a radical change of attitude may be expected in him at once, and the habit of self-abuse will be instantly or rapidly relinquished. Very different is the case of a lad who has long practised masturbation, or who has practised it for some time after the advent of puberty, or who has associated sexual imaginations with the practice. Few such boys conquer the habit at once, however much they desire to, and, if the above conditions co-exist, a boy's progress is very slow, and years may pass without anything approaching cure. If in addition to the temptations from within he has foes also without in the form of companions who sneer at his desire for improvement, controvert the statements made to him, and throw temptation in his way, his chance of cure must be enormously decreased. Of such cases I know nothing; for my experience lies solely among boys who have, outside their own hearts, little to hinder and very much to help. As I have dealt elsewhere with the question of aids to chastity, I will make only a brief reference to it here.

The mind is so much influenced by the body that purity is impossible when the body is unduly indulged. No man exists who could inhale the vapour of chloroform without an irresistible desire to sleep. Under these conditions the strongest will would not avail even if the victim knew that by surrender he was sacrificing everything he reverenced and held dear. The lad past the age of puberty who has much stimulating food, who drinks alcohol, who sleeps in a warm and luxurious bed and occupies it for some time before or after sleep, is certain, even if he takes much exercise, to be tempted irresistibly. Dr. Dukes considers that a heavy meat meal with alcohol shortly before bedtime is in itself sufficient to ensure a lad's fall.

Meanwhile, no abstinence which it not unduly rigorous, can save a boy from impurity if he gets into the habit of exchanging glances with girls who are socially inferior, if he reads suggestive books, looks at stimulating pictures and sights, and falls into the hopeless folly of entertaining sexual thoughts even momentarily. He who has not the strength to tread out a spark is little likely to subdue a conflagration.

The best and most timely teaching will never make carelessness in these matters justifiable, and a boy who has once been corrupted and desires to master his lower nature has no chance of self-conquest unless he gives them his constant and careful attention.

It is very important to fill a boy's leisure with congenial occupation. Idleness and dullness make a boy specially susceptible to temptation. On the other hand, the fond parent who satisfies a boy's every whim and encourages the lad to think that his own enjoyment is the chief thing in life does his utmost to destroy the lad's chance of purity—or, indeed, of any virtue whatever.

Can anything be done for boys and young men who have become the slaves of self-abuse to such an extent that they groan in the words of St. Paul: "The good that I would I do not, but the evil which I would not, that I do.... I delight in the law of God after the inward man, but I see another law in my members warring against the law of my mind and bringing me into captivity to the law of sin which is in my members. O wretched man that I am! who shall deliver me from the body of this death?" Can anything be done for the lad who has become so defiled by lustful thoughts that his utmost efforts fail to carry him forward, and even leave him to sink deeper in the mire. There are many, many such cases, alas! for as Dr. Acton says, "The youth is a dreamer who will open the floodgates of an ocean, and then attempt to prescribe at will a limit to the inundation."

Yes there is a remedy—I believe a specific—which can rapidly and, I think, finally restore strength to the enfeebled will and order the unclean spirit to come out of the man. It is hypnotic suggestion. Let not the reader, however, think that the matter is a simple one. In all ages any great advance in the art of healing has, by the ignorant, been attributed to the powers of darkness. The Divine Healer Himself did not escape from the charge of casting out devils by the prince of the devils, and, while hypnotic suggestion has long been used for therapeutic purposes on the Continent and is now practised in Government institutions there, the doctor or clergyman or teacher who uses it in England runs great risks; for in this subject, as in all others, it is those who are entirely without experience who are most dogmatic.

In the case of the schoolmaster, its use in this connection is practically excluded. If he applies to a parent for permission to use it he probably runs his head against a blank wall of ignorance; for hypnotism, to most people, means a dangerous power by which an unscrupulous, strong-willed Svengali dominates an abnormally weak-willed Trilby whose will continues to grow weaker until the subject becomes a mere automaton; and most of us would rightly prefer that a boy should be his own master—even if he were rushing to headlong ruin—than that he should be the mere puppet of the most saintly man living. The human will is sacred and inviolable, and we do unwisely if we seek to control it or to remove those obstacles from its way by which alone it can gain divine strength. Meanwhile the stimulus by which the mind acquires self-mastery usually comes from without in the form of spiritual inspiration; and to remove from a boy's path an obstacle which blocks it and is entirely beyond his own strength is equally desirable both in the physical and in the spiritual realm. Those who think that without this obstacle a boy's power of self-control is likely to receive insufficient exercise will, of course, object to the instruction advocated in this book. If it is unwise to remove this obstacle from a boy's path it is equally unwise so to instruct him as to prevent the obstacle from arising. In trustworthy hands hypnotic suggestion is a beneficent power which has no dangers and no drawbacks, and to decline to use it is to accept a very serious responsibility.

For the teacher a further difficulty—not to mention that of time—is that, without betraying a boy's confidence or inducing him to allow his admissions to be passed on to his father, it is impossible to give his parents an idea of the urgency of the case.

Altogether the time for hypnotic suggestion in education is not yet, but the day must come when its use is recognised not only in physical cases such as nocturnal emissions and constipation, but in all cases in which the will-power is practically in abeyance, as it is in bad cases of impurity.

For intelligent parents the difficulties are far less, and if any such care to pursue the subject farther, I would refer them to the volume onHypnotism in the People's Books series or to one of the larger medical works on the subject, such as Hypnotism and Suggestion, by Dr. Bernard Hollander.

To those who know boys well and love them much, there is something intensely interesting and pathetic about the spiritual struggle through which they have to pass. The path of self-indulgence seems so obviously the path to happiness; self-denial is so hard and self-control so difficult. "The struggle of the instinct that enjoys and the more noble instinct that aspires" is ever there. The young soul reaches out after good, but its grasp is weak. It needs much enlightenment, much encouragement, much inspiration, much patient tolerance of its faults, much hopeful sympathy with its strivings, if it is ever to attain the good it seeks. In the past it has met, without light or aid, unwarned and unprepared, the deadliest foe which can assail the soul. An appetite which has in all ages debased the weak, wrestled fiercely with the strong, and vanquished at times even the noble, is let loose upon an unwarned, unarmed, defenceless child. Oh, the utter, the utter folly of it!

For life after death the writer has no longing. Immortality, if vouchsafed, appears to him to be a gift to be accepted trustfully and humbly, not to be yearned after with a sort of transcendental egoism. But to him the wish to—

"Join the choir invisible

Of those immortal dead who live again

In minds made better by their presence"

grows ever stronger as the inevitable end draws nearer.

To save young lives from the needless struggles and failures of my own, to secure healthy motherhood or maiden life to some whom lust might otherwise destroy, to add, for some at least, new sanctity to human passion—these have been my hopes in penning the foregoing pages. It has been my privilege and joy, in my own quiet sphere, to preserve boys from corruption and to restore the impure to cleanness of heart. I am deeply grateful for the opportunity these pages afford of extending this delightful work. When the hand which writes these lines has long been cold in death, may the message which it speeds this day breathe peace and strength into many an eager heart.